What Did Jesus Say?

Daily Devotional and Study Guide

Paul G. Dixon

ISBN

CONTENTS

AKNOWLEDGEMENTS

For God, my Father and Jesus, my Savior: *"O give thanks unto the LORD; for he is good: because his mercy endureth forever."* Psalm 118:1

To my wife, Dr. Cindy S. Dixon, for her love and devotion and to all of my family!

Special Thanks:

To Brother Andrews for his encouragement and advice.

A. R. Dixon, Austin Ellis, D. F. Mitchell, Dr. Cindy S. Dixon, Gay McCabe, Sharon S. Cook.....editing

Mary Haney......cover design

INTRODUCTION

This study is an excellent way to begin one's spiritual journey by reading and considering scripture through Matthew, Mark, Luke, and John. The goal of this study guide is to help readers navigate through all four gospel accounts. All scripture references are in the King James Version, unless otherwise noted. The brief commentaries will help students at any familiarity level, whether beginning, intermediate, or experienced. Since all four gospels are used, some ideas are repeated. After each week, the student should be able to list at least seven specific things that Jesus said from the prior week's lessons.

Please note that since Jesus is the author of the entire New Testament, his message encompasses far more than just the words printed in red. This guide should not replace consistent reading of God's Word; instead, it should promote a consistent, daily period of devotion and additional learning alongside one's readings. Wider margins and additional space have been provided so that the guide can be used as a notebook as well as a daily prayer journal. The writer hopes that designing a devotional book in this way has promoted, rather than hindered, its ease of use. Read the scriptures first, before each devotional. Use the open-ended meditations to prompt more study. Always be sure your answers are Biblical. Remember to *"Prove all things; hold fast that which is good"* (1 Thessalonians 5:21).

Week 1
What Do You Seek?

John 1:29-38

John invites his readers to consider God's sacrifice when he first introduces Jesus in John 1:29. Afterwards, Jesus' first recorded words are in the form of a question in John 1:38: *"What seek ye?"* Read it slowly a few times and think about what it would have been like to be there, hearing this question from Jesus himself. The Master teaches that those who follow him should look within their own hearts to know the real purpose of their discipleship. Later, Jesus gives his followers insight as to how their priorities are to be aligned when he says, *"Seek ye first the kingdom of God, and His righteousness ....."* (KJV, Matthew 6:33).

Meditation: What happened to convince many of John's disciples to become disciples of Jesus?

Prayer: Dear Lord, teach us to follow thy son Jesus!

Come and See!
John 1:37-42

The Lord invites all disciples to begin their walk by seeing how frugally he lived. He chose to forgo the riches of heaven and earth to walk the dusty roads of Palestine among men. He noted that foxes had holes and the birds of the air had nests, and yet the Son of man had no earthly residence (Matthew 8:20). Knowing this world is not our destined home causes us to center our attention on the path prepared for us by our Savior rather than focusing on many of life's challenges or pleasures that might distract us.

Meditation: What must we decide to do before we are ready to *"come and see"* where Jesus is? Does walking with Jesus come as a result of evidence? (See Hebrews 11:1.)

Prayer: Guide me today, oh thou Great Jehovah. Our Father, begin to create in me a new heart.

Follow Me
John 1:43-46

Every disciple's life begins here: there are mountains to climb, streams to cross, and valleys to endure, yet our eyes are to look steadily to Jesus with our footsteps in his. Finding dependable fellow Christians who edify us will help us on our spiritual journey and keep us on the right track. In verse 46, Philip says to Nathanael the same thing Jesus had earlier said to Simon Peter: *"Come and see."* Jesus' influence is clearly seen by noticing that these same men had already begun to follow Jesus' words and examples.

Meditation: What often happens when we become weary on our spiritual journey? When following Jesus, how often should we be expected to carry our cross?

Prayer: Help me, Oh Lord, to take up my cross daily and follow you. Father, accept thou my thanks for the day with all of its glory!

Let It Be This Way
Matthew 3:15; Mark 16:16; 1 Peter 3:21; Acts 8:38-39

Jesus was baptized through immersion by his cousin, John the Baptizer. But if Jesus had no sins, why was there a need for him to be immersed? Surely it was to please his heavenly Father, to fulfill the scriptures concerning him, and to set an example for us by showing what we should do if we ourselves want to please the Father. Since Jesus had no sins, some make the wrongful claim that baptism's purpose today is not to cleanse a person from sin, and is instead, merely a public and ritualistic expression of the fact that a person is already cleansed. While this may sound convincing, it is a dangerous exaggeration and is quite far from the truth. Later in scripture, we see a person being baptized for the express purpose of washing his sins away. (See Acts 22:16.)

Meditation: Is baptism necessary for a person to be saved today? Since Jesus was immersed in the waters of the Jordan River, are we also to be immersed in a river? Do the scriptures reveal one is saved before or after baptism?

Prayer: Lord, help me to learn the truth that makes men free! Lord, let me walk closer to thee each day!

Not by Bread Alone!
Matthew 4:1-11

While Jesus was combatting his many temptations in the wilderness, he was showing us how we can protect ourselves from the enemy. Through his craftiness, Satan waited until Jesus was weak from hunger, tempting him with food when he had not eaten for 40 days. Jesus used scripture against each of the devil's attempts. These useful examples can help us deal with our spiritual battles as we understand that our enemy will look for our vulnerabilities when casting his evil net. Christians can have the ultimate confidence that comes with knowing we can do all things through Christ who strengthens us (Philippians 4:13).

Meditation: Most of us experience hunger at least once each day, but do we experience spiritual hunger? How often should we include spiritual food in our diet? How long can the average person survive without food? What is different about spiritual food when considering one's spiritual survival?

Prayer: Oh God! Teach us how to do battle with Satan while loving our enemies! Help us to succeed in our fights of faith.

Get Behind Me, Satan!
Luke 4:1-13

Our allegiance must solely be to the one and only true God. Jesus teaches his followers how to avoid the snares of our enemy, Satan. It is only when we are swiftly putting the devil behind us that we are choosing wisely. Successful travelers of life are those who serve the one true Master. Jesus later makes it known that it is impossible to serve or follow two opposing masters. He illustrates this principle in Matthew 7:24-29 when he tells of the wise man who built his house on the rock and the foolish man who built his house on the sand.

Meditation: When people fall into temptation, are they then servants of Satan? How does Satan become one's spiritual father, master, or leader?

Prayer: Oh God, help us to be more like our Savior! Teach us, oh Father, to serve the true Master!

Save Yourselves
Luke 4:12; 8:4-18, Acts 2:40

Sadly, it seems some unsaved and or "unchurched" people are saying, "If the Lord can catch me, he can have me. If I can slow down long enough to catch my breath, then I might have time to become his disciple." This way of thinking is a common one. It alludes to how busy and burdened everyone always is with the struggles of this life. The time spent with hobbies, recreations, and the pursuit of wealth leave many devoid of a fulfilling spiritual life. They think that time does not allow for things apart from those habitual endeavors which seem to plague us all and do not excuse any of us. Many make it quite difficult for the Lord to take priority, and as a result, they keep their hearts hardened toward him. They risk their souls despite the assurance of impending death for all.

Meditation: What are some of the things that can so easily sway one's attention away from important spiritual matters?

Prayer: Dear Lord, don't allow me to be too distracted from spiritual matters. Oh Father, keep me always in thy love!

Week 2

He Has Sent Me to Preach

Luke 4:18-21; John 14:6; Matthew 7:13,14

Our Lord Jesus was given the full measure of the Spirit and all knowledge of truth. His Father wanted him to share the good news to the poor, tell prisoners of the ultimate freedom, restore sight to the blind, and give liberty to all that were treated unjustly. Isaiah is quoted as having said that we are like *"sheep that have gone astray."* People today understandably need a clear path to follow, and that path is distinctly revealed in scripture. It is described as the straight and narrow way that leads to life in Matthew 7:13, 14. It is very different than the broad way described in the same passage that leads to destruction and ruin.

Meditation: In John 14:6, Jesus declared He was *"the way"* and *"the truth"* that leads to God. So what is necessary for us to see the truth and choose the path that ensures heaven as our destination?

Prayer: Dearest Lord, help me to find the Way that is right and true. Righteous Father, I wish to tread the one true path.

God's Kingdom Is Near
Mark 1:15; Matthew 16:18; Matthew 28:19-20

"The kingdom of God is at hand . . ." (Mark 1:15). Mark writes that the long-awaited kingdom would no longer be a prospect of the future, but would become a reality of the present! This is Jesus' first statement, written by Mark and shows us that according to God's calendar, the kingdom, being the Lord's church was near. Knowing that his promised church, the kingdom would soon arrive, Jesus issued commands that his followers could obey to be saved and become members. Christ's disciples would hear the gospel and *"believe," "repent," "confess"* and then *"be baptized"* (Mark 16:16; cf. Acts 2:38). Since saved individuals were actively being added to the church in Acts 2:47, the text clearly proves the church's existence at that time. It was on the Day of Pentecost, a Sunday morning, that about 3,000 people responded favorably to the gospel of Jesus Christ, taking up brotherhood one with another. They

happily met the Lord's conditions in order to receive and accept the good news of his grace. The good news was, just as it is now, the powerful message of mankind's redemption.

Meditation: Why does God have a plan of salvation? What are the steps that we must adhere to before being considered saved? What are those steps found in the passages of the Book of Acts according to the Apostles?

Prayer: Lord, teach us to make all the necessary changes required to please thee. Teach us to seek only the path of true righteousness and not one that is false.

Physician, Heal Yourself!
Luke 4:22-23; Matthew 27:39-44

Jesus is described as a physician, but he was not your typical general practitioner. He was instead the Great Physician, healing us from sin and saving our souls! Jesus here refers to the certainty of his cross and eventual death thereon, telling of how scoffers would disrespect him and want to see a sign from him when they had heard the reports of miracles in other places. They would prompt him to do them on demand. Those attendants at his death, mocking him while he hung suspended on his cross, essentially offered to Jesus the following proposition: "If you will perform a miracle to save yourself and come down from the cross, we will believe." Jesus did not come down from the cross, but he did come forth from the tomb. Today, Jesus invites us to review the evidence of his resurrection and believe, to come to him from out of this dark world so that he can translate us into his kingdom of light, thus saving us through the power of the gospel.

Meditation: Is it possible that people today are also waiting for some sign to convince them to make up their minds to seek and follow him? Did Jesus ever promise to send signs such as special feelings so that people would choose him?

Prayer: Our Lord, may we follow thee wherever you lead us! Teach us how to best seek thy path.

Not Accepted at Home
Luke 4:24-30

It was Jesus' custom to do fewer signs in those places where his divinity was most doubted. It appears that Jesus was accepted in other cities and places more than he ever was in his own community. Joseph, his earthly father, was a carpenter; and most likely, Jesus was his apprentice. Having witnessed his childhood and knowing of his earthly family and his father's trade, many were blind to the truth of his identity. Jesus was indeed the Christ and was much more than a mere carpenter. Phillip said, *"We have found the Messiah."* Nicodemus, who came to Jesus at night, obviously knew Jesus was more than just a man, and so proclaimed him as a teacher sent from God.

13

Meditation: Why are missionaries often more accepted in foreign places than they are in their home countries? Evangelists have spread the good news of mankind's redemption over many years. Name some ways to take the message of the cross far and wide to other nations.

Prayer: Lord, teach us to carry thy message to our neighbors, whether domestic or otherwise. Oh God, we give thanks to you for our many countless opportunities to introduce thee to others.

Be Quiet and Come Out
Luke 4:33-37; 1 Cor. 5:7; Romans 6:4-7

With a simple command, *"Be quiet and come out,"* Jesus rebuked and removed a devil that had possession of a man in Luke 4:35. Though people are tempted today, demon possession has vanished in its entirety, no longer afflicting men as it once did. The Lord now commands sinners to stop giving their lives to Satan, putting to death their *"old man"* (self) through repentance and baptism. As such, we would do well to remember this when next we are inevitably tempted. Jesus told the unclean spirit to *"be quiet" (NKJV)*. Even today, being quiet is required of us in some parts of our worship. Being quiet calms us when we join in prayer and aids us when we observe the Lord's Supper. In 1 Corinthians 14:30, women are told to be silent in the assemblies. Later, the apostle Paul would write in Romans 6:4-7 that we are to crucify our *"old man"* to become a new man in Christ. This new person should always *"lead a quiet and peaceable life in all godliness and honesty"* (1

14

Timothy 2:2). The new life is to be quite different from the old.

Meditation: Since the demon – having a nature for the darkest of intentions – was instructed to be quiet, shouldn't a false teacher today follow that same instruction?

Prayer: Lord, help us to learn how to crucify the *"old man"* and become a new person. Teach us to forget the cares of the past and press forward with a desire for what is true.

Launch out into the Deep
Luke 5:1-10; Matthew 4:18-22

In these passages, the Lord calls on his disciples to practice their faith by fishing in deeper waters. It is remarkable that, for those who decide to follow Jesus, the failures of their past do not predict the success of their future. Peter shares his failures with the Lord in Luke 5:5. They had fished all night without success, but Peter notes that at Jesus' word, they will try once more. The tremendous success they find through their obedience is a miracle and nothing short of amazing. They caught so many fish that their boats overflowed and began to sink! Afterwards, Jesus tells them of a more worthy pursuit than catching fish: catching men! Jesus showed his disciples how to become fishers of men, reeling in men and women from the depths of a sinful and broken world, as was Jesus' mission. Jesus came to seek and save the lost, and his compassion and concerns are ever present as he calls disciples to help him accomplish this great and global task. A fisher of men is committed for life to help save others.

Meditation: If we allow them to, past failures can limit our faith and hinder our spiritual progress. How can we let go of the past and move forward? What was Jesus teaching the disciples by filling both boats with fish? What did the disciples learn that day about who Jesus was?

Prayer: Lord, help us to trust that when we listen to thee, things will improve. Help us realize that our past failures do not need to diminish the brighter days we have ahead.

You Will See Angels
John 1: 47-51; Acts 2:37-38, 41

Without doubt, the apostles and disciples of Jesus witnessed many strange and wonderful things. They began seeing more than simply what was on the surface, a clear indication that they were spending time with the Son of God. It is apparent to us that they witnessed many miracles, signs, and wonders! After Jesus' death on the cross, burial, and resurrection, they saw Christ's church for the very first time on Pentecost, the Sunday morning described in Acts 2:1-41. That same day, they witnessed about 3,000 baptized into Christ and thereby added to the Lord's body, the church, with more responding every day.

Meditation: Though we no longer witness miracles, what are some special things that Christians can see today?

Prayer: Lord, please, supplement my unbelief! Oh Father, guide me to learn more about Jesus' one, true church.

Week 3
Fill the Water Pots!
John 2:1-11

At a wedding in Cana, Jesus is asked to provide wine for the guests. Some today question whether the wine was fermented wine. However, there are several good reasons to believe that the wine Jesus made on this occasion was purely grape juice. The statement, *"after the manner of the purifying of the Jews"* shows the time of this wedding to be during the Jew's purification period. Immediately before the Passover, Jews were forbidden to partake of any substance containing leaven (Exodus 12:15). It was not that the leaven itself was sinful, but that it represented a foreign substance mixed into a purer one. Fermented wine would have been impure for the same reason: it contains ethyl alcohol, a poison. Alcohol is defined as *"a colorless volatile flammable liquid (C_2H_5OH)"* (American Heritage Dictionary). Alcohol is a drug and a poison. Consuming it involves a risk that increases with the amount consumed-the only absolutely safe level is zero (Davey).

It would not be reasonable to believe that Jesus turned the water in the six containers—water which would have been used for purification purposes—into a poisonous substance. Neither would he have contributed willingly to the drunkenness of the guests, which was strictly forbidden under Jewish law.

Meditation: Some use this miracle to try to condone the activity of social drinking, but why? Does social drinking harm or enhance a Christian's influence? What other scriptures might be considered?

Prayer: Dear Lord, may we remember to respect thee and thy church. Oh God our Father, let us love and hate the same things that you do! May our influence always be for good.

My Father's House
John 2:13-22; Acts 2:1-47; 1 Timothy 3:15

Understandably, Jesus was very protective of his Father's house, for it was never meant to be a house of merchandise. Later, after Christ's death, burial, and resurrection, the house of God would also be Christ's house, or the church of Christ. Jesus, speaking of his own body as if it were a temple, foretells of his Father's house becoming his church. It would require his death by crucifixion. God's house still exists today; it remains the church of Christ, an accurate expression that the apostle Paul uses in his letter to the Romans (Romans 16:16). The church is still to be a house of praise, devotion, and worship even today.

God has always wanted true worship (John 4:24) and love (Hebrews 13:1) in the church.

Our Lord expressed the kind of love he wants in his church with the death of his only begotten Son. Three days after his death, the Lord Jesus arose from the tomb and commissioned his disciples to preach the gospel to the entire world. The gospel that they taught included the death, burial, and resurrection of Jesus Christ. The love story of the cross was preached like never before in the first century, beginning on that first day of the week, Sunday, the Day of Pentecost (Acts 2:1-41). Men and women responded in obedience to the gospel because of Peter's answer to the most important question anyone has ever asked. (See Acts 2:37.)

Meditation: What promise do Christians have today that they too will be raised up from death into life, just as Christ? How and when does one enter into eternal life? Is it immediately after drawing the last breath? Would it be possible for someone to represent God's church today as a house of trade? What proof do we have that this happens today?

Prayer: Dear Lord, help me to respond favorably to the message of the cross. Father, let my faith in thee grow more each day.

Power to Forgive Sins
Luke 5:16-26

Jesus asked in Luke 5:16-26 what was easier to say, *"Thy sins be forgiven thee; or to say, rise up and walk?"* (Luke 5:23). Every sinner can trust today that Jesus has the power to forgive sins. That power could be observed when someone was healed. Testimony of his supernatural healing is found time and time again in the scriptures. It is interesting to observe that Jesus' statement, *"rise up and walk"* also has a spiritual meaning, for we rise up from baptism and then walk in *"newness of life"* (Romans 6:3-4). This is God's plan for all mankind, the epitome of truth itself.

Meditation: Jesus asked, *"What reason ye in your hearts?"* (Luke 5:22). Do you feel it is truly necessary for us to find reasons for the many good works that the Lord chose to do, or is it more important for us to understand the authority by which he did them?

Prayer: Lord, teach us to number our many countless blessings. Dear God, show us those who are ready to receive your gospel.

Humble in Spirit
Matthew 5:3; Luke 6:20

It is quite possible to be poor and yet rich at the same time; in fact, Jesus recommends it! Acknowledging our spiritual emptiness is difficult, but it's an important first step and a vital step toward repairing a spiritual relationship with the Creator or beginning a new one. How can a disciple of Christ ever hope to grow, mature, and be rich in faith if he does not feel a need for the Lord in his life?

Meditation: What is the spiritual blessing experienced by those who have knowledge of the truth? (See John 8:32.)

Prayer: Lord, may we reach more of our potential while daily looking to thee. Please open our eyes and hearts that we may see and know ourselves clearly.

Those Who Mourn
Matthew 5:4; Job 42

Although faithful Christians are promised an abundant life, we are not promised a life totally free of sorrow and suffering while we toil in the here and now. And though His *"yoke is easy and his burden light,"* there will be struggles and hardships along life's weary way. Assuredly, God is the God of all comfort; he can and will make things better for us with time. His promises are predicated through his Son Jesus Christ through whom all things are possible!

Meditation: What comforts and strengths can the Lord provide us with today?

Prayer: Lord, please help me in all my afflictions. Teach me to be always content with what I have.

Blessed Are the Meek
Matthew 5:5; Numbers 12:3

Christians should divest themselves of all foolish pride and invest in God. This will ensure that the Christian has an eternal inheritance. Moses was a very meek man and became one of the Lord's greatest leaders (Joshua 1:16-17). His example of humility remains one of the best to show us how God promotes those who will humble themselves in his sight.

Meditation: Does meek mean weak? Is there anything at all a person should be unwilling to give up to be able to follow Christ?

Prayer: Lord, please show us how to be our best selves. Help us discover what we should consider giving up for thee.

Hunger and Thirst
Matthew 5:6; 2 Timothy 2:15

Choosing a healthy spiritual diet leads one to spiritual fulfillment. It can add both health and prosperity to one's soul and create a life of abundance. Those who search the Word of God for salvation will find a blessing not found anywhere else.

Meditation: How often should one read the Bible? Are there any passages that reflect on the frequency at which a reader can acquire wisdom and knowledge from God?

Prayer: Lord, I want to be filled spiritually. Let me hunger and thirst always for thy word.

Week 4

Blessed Are the Merciful

Matthew 5:7; Luke 23:34

Forgiving others of their personal offences, overlooking minor disagreements, and forgiving debts are all examples of having mercy. Showing mercy to others is of vital importance in every community. By demonstrating mercy to others, God's love for mankind is shown through his children. After all, how else can one show others the alluring mercy of the one true God? The failure to properly teach mercy begins within our own families. Moments of mercy are always a blessing both to the giver and to the receiver.

Meditation: What promise can the merciful expect from God? In what ways do we receive mercy?

Prayer: Father, forgive us our debts as we forgive our debtors. Help us to be more merciful!

Pure of Heart
Matthew 5:8; James 1:27; James 4:8

God is pure and everyone who desires to be like God is to be pure in heart. Such purity requires self-examination and a commitment to purge oneself of anything that God hates. Hating what God hates and loving what God loves is absolutely necessary to be like God, but it is not all done immediately. It is not achieved instantaneously, but by taking one moment, one step, and one day at a time. For example, resisting a temptation strengthens us to resist the next one and the one after that. Hearts become purer as our resistance to temptation grows stronger.

Meditation: What are some practical solutions for creating a pure heart? Can the heart ever become so calloused that it can't become pure again?

Prayer: Lord, create in me a clean heart! My heart is hard, yet may it be soft once more!

Peacemakers
Matthew 5:9; 2 Timothy 2:22-26

A blessing is ascribed to all who work to settle their differences peacefully instead of through petty strife, arguments, and fights. Followers of Christ should seek first to pursue true peace before expecting to help others find it. True and lasting peace is a gift through obedience and adherence to the gospel of Jesus Christ. We must, therefore, be cleansed of all unrighteousness and be washed in the blood of the

Lamb for the remission of our sins, whereby every troubled conscience is made clean. Priceless is a godly conscience cleansed and contented by his perfect peace!

Meditation: If God's peace passes all understanding, is it at all possible to understand God's peace?

Prayer: Lord, we need peace in our lives! Show us thy perfect peace in the gospel and make us peacemakers!

Be Exceedingly Glad
Matthew 5:10-12; Luke 6:22-26; 2 Timothy 3:11-12

The Lord reminds us that just as the people of his day led him to the cross amidst mockery and scorn, people today will jeer at his followers as they carry their crosses for Him. Suffering for wrongdoing is expected, and suffering patiently while doing well is honorable and righteous. It is interesting to observe that the Lord says to *"rejoice and be exceedingly glad"* in these circumstances, a reaction quite different from that which one often sees. This might seem an impossible task until one pauses to consider how great the reward is which awaits every faithful child of God.

Meditation: What kinds of persecutions might a Christian suffer today? What are some biblical examples of great persecution suffered by righteous people?

Prayer: Lord, strengthen my resolve, so that I may try to be more like thee. Let me hide my weakness within the strength of thy might.

Salt of the Earth
Matthew 5:13; John 17:1-10

Food without salt has less flavor, making it bland to the taste. Food with salt has more flavor and creates thirst. Likewise, a Christian without salt will lose his or her influence. The Christian's speech is to be generously seasoned with salt. Christians are always hopeful that their words are well received by others as they share their faith. Still, some will not believe and others will even persecute. Displays of anger, tasteless jokes, and hurtful innuendos should be avoided by all means necessary if Christians ever hope to express sincerity to others and win souls for Christ. Lewd expressions only damage one's reputation and make one seem worldly.

Meditation: How does a Christian retain saltiness? How would a Christian lose saltiness?

Prayer: Lord, help me to stand up in this world full of sin. Teach me what it means to be the salt of the earth.

Light of the World
Matthew 5:14-15; John 8:12; 1 John 1:7-10

Christians are lights in this dark and sinful world. Jesus said we are a city that is set on a hill to be seen by everyone. We use the influence that we have to lead the lost out of sin. The darker the world becomes, the brighter a Christian's light will need to shine. Our lights shimmer from our good works that we use to help point people to Christ and his cross; thereby, God is glorified among men!

Meditation: What is the sole purpose of a lighthouse? A candle? A Christian?

Prayer: Lord, help us to be a light to others. Teach us how to keep our light shining brightly!

Let Your Light so Shine
Matthew 5:16; John 15:1-10

Jesus said that *"by their fruits you will know them."* Good works are indicative of a Christian who lets his light shine. Christ also referred to good works as good fruit, something only good trees will produce. Corrupt trees also produce fruit. The fruits of wicked men are easily discovered to be wicked. Likewise, the fruits of righteous men accordingly are righteous. When our fruit is good, we are letting our lights shine.

Meditation: What are some good works that others should see of a Christian? Are belief, repentance, confession, and baptism all solely matters of faith, or are they good works as well?

Prayer: Lord, help me to be a good tree. Teach me how to produce good fruits.

Week 5

Not to Destroy, but to Fulfill
Matthew 5:17-18; Hebrews 8-9

The Ten Commandments and all of the Old Law ordinances were written exclusively for the Jewish nation, the children of Israel, long before Jesus' death on the cross. The New Testament, however, is written for Christians who, because of the cross, are now the redeemed: God's brand-new Israel. *"Think not that I am come to destroy the law, or the prophets: I am not come to destroy, but to fulfill"* (Matthew 5:17). Therefore, the Old Testament is now *"fulfilled"* or filled full.

Meditation: What does it mean to fulfill something? Which law was the thief on the cross to obey: the old or the new?

Prayer: Lord, help us to obey all that you command today. Teach us to observe the law that was meant for us.

Righteousness Excels
Matthew 5:19-20; 2 Timothy 4: 1-5

Some seem righteous, while others are righteous. There were those in Jesus' day that had a form of public religiosity, yet they were not righteous. Jesus said, some honored him with their mouths, but their hearts were far from Him. All true Christians will be rewarded now in this lifetime and in the next. A crown of glory in the life hereafter is promised to all of God's good and faithful servants.

"For I say unto you, that except your righteousness shall exceed the righteousness of the scribes and Pharisees, ye shall in no case enter into the kingdom of heaven" (Matthew 5:20).

Meditation: Does the Bible speak of false brethren? What did Jesus mean when he warned his disciples to *"beware of the leaven of the Pharisees"?*

Prayer: Lord, help my righteousness to be acceptable to thee. May I come to know what is required of me by thee.

Angry without Cause
Matthew 5:21-22; Hebrews 13:1;
Matthew 12:36-37

"But I say unto you, that whosoever is angry with his brother without a cause shall be in danger of the judgment: and whosoever shall say to his brother, Raca, shall be in danger of the council; but whosoever

shall say, Thou fool, shall be in danger of hell fire" (Matthew 5:22). It is possible to be angry and not sin, but it is also easy to become angry and say something that we might later regret. What we say and how we say it certainly can affect where we will spend eternity. How people think and behave towards their fellow brethren is vital to their inheritance in the afterlife. *"Let brotherly love continue"* (Hebrews 13:1).

Meditation: Why is it so important to guard our language? Why is it particularly difficult to watch what we say when we are angry? Could a misstep in this area potentially cause someone to lose his or her soul?

Prayer: Lord, please help me to improve my speech. Teach me to be slow to anger and quick to listen.

Gifts to the Altar
Matthew 5:23-24; Hebrews 13:1

"Therefore if thou bring thy gift to the altar, and there rememberest that thy brother hath ought against thee; Leave there thy gift before the altar, and go thy way; first be reconciled to thy brother, and then come and offer thy gift" (Matthew 5:23-24). Some are well-meaning and hope to mend their relationships simply by giving a heartfelt gift. They feel that an unselfish deed will resolve any conflict between themselves and a brother. Any wrong will then just go away and be forgotten. But Jesus says that in such cases, we should pursue reconciliation with our brother first, so that what is then done for the Lord can be offered without hypocrisy. A greater gift is thereby given

when it is paired with positive relationships with our brethren, thereby showing God our love for him.

Meditation: Does reconciliation with God first require reconciliation with one another? Or is the reverse true?

Prayer: Lord, help us to love our brothers more. Teach us to adore thee and our savior, Jesus Christ!

Agree with Thine Adversary
Matthew 5:25-26

"Agree with thine adversary quickly . . ." (Matthew 5:25). Rocking "aft and bow" in a wind tossed vessel can cause someone to lose his or her sense of balance and thus fall. Sometimes it is wise to sit still and let the Lord first calm the seas. Procrastinating with some problems may prove to be prudent, however many need to be solved quickly and decisively. Just remember, when choosing what is best, it is always wise to trust the Lord!

Meditation: If a Christian frequently expresses himself or herself openly and outwardly, should that person not also expect frequent disagreements, trials, and persecutions? Is there ever a time that a Christian should remain utterly quiet?

Prayer: Dear Lord, teach us to speak with wisdom. Help us to know how we should best express ourselves towards thee and others.

Looking at a Woman
Matthew 5:27-28; Job 31:1

"But I say unto you, that whosoever looketh on a woman to lust after her hath committed adultery with her already in his heart" (Matthew 5:28). Righteous Job long ago made a covenant with his eyes. He did not want to sin against God with the *"lust of the eye."* People are visual beings, especially men who may look at women with impure motives. We live in an immodest society, so keeping oneself pure can, at times, be extremely difficult; but it is absolutely necessary in order to please the Lord, finish the race in earnest, and win the everlasting crown.

Meditation: Why is committing adultery in one's heart not the same as physical fornication? When can a wife rightfully divorce her husband, based on scripture? Study 1 Corinthians 6:15-20.

Prayer: Lord, help us to set our attention to eternal things. Teach us to focus on only those things that can save us.

Our Own Worst Enemy
Matthew 5:29-30; Romans 7:14-25

"And if thy right eye offend thee . . ." (Matthew 5:29). One of the ways we are tempted is through our eyes. The lust of the eyes has been around for a long time. Jesus said that if our eye was causing us to stumble and there was any chance we would be lost from it,

then take it out and throw it away. It would be better to do that than to be entirely lost. Though the Lord is compassionate and always provides his children with a way to escape each temptation (1 Corinthians 10:13), there is always a danger of giving in to temptation. Without self-discipline, we often end up being our own worst enemies. Developing some self-control upon the strength and trust of the Lord is the key to fighting temptations. Being strong in the Lord will help us take the good fight to the next level.

Meditation: If the Apostle Paul himself struggled against sin, doesn't it make sense that all Christians will do battle with temptation? What armor does the Lord provide?

Prayer: Lord, help us to prepare ourselves for the fight. Assist us as we resist our common enemy.

Week 6
A Scriptural Divorce
Matthew 5:31-32; Matthew 19:3-12;
1 Corinthians 7:1-40

"But I say unto you, That whosoever shall put away his wife, saving for the cause of fornication, causeth her to commit adultery: and whosoever shall marry her that is divorced committeth adultery" (Matthew 5:32). A good marriage is never an accident! Marriage is to be a lifelong commitment between a man and woman. Jesus starts this sentence in Matthew 5:32 with the phrase *"but I say unto you,"* making what follows next

applicable to all Christians past and present, regardless of the audience at the time. Jesus is not here (or in Matthew 19:9) permitting divorce so long as a divorcee never remarries, as many have claimed. He is only permitting marriage in the specific case of a scriptural divorce. Many have been successful in garnering legal approval for their divorces, but have they received them with the Lord's stamp of approval? When the divorce violates Matthew 19:9, then it is achieved on a societal level and never on a spiritual level. Biblically speaking, the bond of husband and wife is not easily broken and will continue even when some think it has been severed. *"What therefore God hath joined together, let not man put asunder"* (Matthew 19:6).

Meditation: In Matthew 19:7 the Pharisees asked, *"Why did Moses then command to give a writing of divorcement, and to put her away?"* How did Jesus answer?

Prayer: Lord, help us to hold on to our marital and spiritual commitments. Instill in us a will to love our spouses through the good and the bad.

Good Communication
Matthew 5:33-37; Ephesians 4:29

"But let your communication be, Yea, yea; Nay, nay . . ." (Matthew 5:37). It is becoming more common by the day to hear empty promises, euphemisms, and meaningless gestures of assurance. For example, the phrase "O my God" is acceptable when used in praying or singing praises to God. However, at this

present time, the phrase has become a popular exclamation often abbreviated in social media as OMG. When used thoughtlessly and often rudely, the danger is very real that God's name is taken in vain. People judge us by our words, whether we are speaking casually or making promises. The old saying, "A man's word is his bond," still applies. Without doubt, a Christian should mean what he says and say only what he means, no more and no less and always with respect for God.

Meditation: If it is wrong to curse and take God's name in vain, then is it ever wrong to agree to listen to it, such as with a group of friends or listen to it in a movie?

Prayer: Lord, help us to not take thy name in vain. Teach us to think before we speak, O God.

Turn the Other Cheek
Matthew 5:38-40

"... *but whosoever shall smite thee on thy right cheek, turn to him the other also*" (Matthew 5:39). Christians put their self-control on display constantly, as they often find themselves in difficult situations of potential character assassination and personal verbal abuse. I once read about a man who turned the other cheek after someone struck his face. After receiving the second blow, however, the man abandoned all restraint and matched the violence of the one who had assaulted him. When he was asked later why he had acted in this peculiar way, he conveyed that the

Lord had not told him what to do after he had turned the other cheek the first time. Obviously, this honest yet misguided person did not understand the principle that Jesus was teaching.

Meditation: What are some examples of how a person might turn the other cheek? Would this principle be popular if ever depicted in a modern-day western show?

Prayer: Lord, permit us to learn self-control. Help us remember not to retaliate but to trust in thee.

Going the Second Mile
Matthew 5:41

"And whosoever shall compel thee to go a mile, go with him twain" (Matthew 5:41). The "two-mile" service plan provides the child of God with many blessings. No one could know for certain how many Roman citizens and soldiers in the first century were beneficiaries of "second-mile" service, but one can confidently assume that many disciples of Christ took their Master's teaching to heart. People were probably astonished at this strange, yet inspiring Christian attitude, and perhaps some entertained the thought of becoming Christians themselves. Today, going the second mile is one of the best ways that Christians can let their lights shine.

Meditation: When a Roman soldier witnessed a Christian going far beyond what he or she was compelled to go, what thoughts about Christians do you think it produced within them? Today when a business owner adopts the principle of doing a little extra for his customers, what good does that promote?

Prayer: Lord, teach us how to go the second mile for thee. O God, thank you for all of our opportunities for good.

Give to Him That Asks
Matthew 5:42; Luke 6:27-32

"Give to him that asketh thee, and from him that would borrow of thee turn not thou away" (Matthew 5:42). A Christian's refusal to give or to lend to others sends the wrong message. Christians should not be stingy, uncaring, or unloving. Certainly, no one can oblige everyone every time, but there will be opportunities when giving would be within one's means, even if it means taking a momentary loss. Remember, Joseph was praised when he opened the storehouses in Egypt and sold corn during the famine. When Christians lend to others, it improves their standing in the community. Though our motivation is one of love, it might be that one day we find ourselves needing a helping hand. The instruction explained in Galatians 6:10 exhorts Christians to use their opportunities to do good for others.

Meditation: How do we benefit when we comply with Jesus' teaching about lending?

Prayer: Lord, teach us not to be selfish with our resources. Help us to delight in sharing with others.

Love Your Enemies
Matthew 5:43-47; Luke 6:27-36

"But I say unto you, Love your enemies, bless them that curse you, do good to them that hate you, and pray for them which despitefully use you, and persecute you" (Matthew 5:44). Christians are not immune to the harmful proliferation of payback and revenge that is common even among brothers and sisters in Christ. Instead of strategizing how we will strike back to get even with our offenders, would it not be better to simply pray for them? Although praying for our offenders may be difficult, a true child of God will find benefit from the practice, perhaps even improving their own temperaments.

Meditation: Christ forgave his persecutors out of love when he prayed for those who placed him on the cross. How might we show love in the face of those who hate us today?

Prayer: O Lord, help me to love my enemies. Show me how to love those who hate me.

Be Perfect
Matthew 5:48; Luke 6:35; 1 John 1:7-10

"Be ye therefore perfect, even as your Father which is in heaven is perfect" (Matthew 5:48). The term "perfect" has two meanings in the New Testament. One definition of perfection defines a condition of being sinless, like Jesus. Note, however, that to live in a perfect condition without ever committing a sin is

quite impossible for mankind. The only other possible definition of perfection equates to meaning "one who is forgiven" and therefore is blameless, or perfect. All must achieve this latter state, in order to enter heaven. When Christians place themselves in the safety of the Lord's arms by entering into the covenant of Christ through the gospel's plan for salvation, they then become a *"new creature"* in the sight of God. A person saved in Christ is, in a sense, perfect in the eyes of the Lord because that person can continue to be forgiven.

Meditation: Are there any requirements that must be satisfied before we can be forgiven by God? If so, is it possible to be forgiven without meeting those requirements?

Prayer: Lord, teach us to be more like Christ. By your grace, forgive us our numerous trespasses!

Week 7

Best to Give without a Trumpet
Matthew 6:1-4; 2 Corinthians 9:7

"Take heed that ye do not your alms before men, to be seen of them: otherwise ye have no reward of your Father which is in heaven" (Matthew 6:1). Proper motives and attitudes toward Christian giving are as important as the gifts themselves. Giving only to receive praise from others causes contributors to miss out on a greater blessing. When given with a pure heart, a gift brings a blessing to both the giver and receiver. Are you noticing a trend? 2 Corinthians

9:7 tells of how God *"loveth a cheerful giver,"* so remember to give cheerfully and out of love.

Meditation: Why did Jesus teach that some would not enter heaven though they gave many gifts?

Prayer: Lord, teach us to give with a pure heart. As we offer up our gifts, may we not forget all the many blessings we have ourselves been gifted.

Praying like a Hypocrite
Matthew 6:5; Luke 6:35; James 4:1-3

"And when thou prayest, thou shalt not be as the hypocrites are: for they love to pray standing in the synagogues and in the corners of the streets, that they may be seen of men. Verily I say unto you, They have their reward" (Matthew 6:5). Christians must pray with proper motives. We should never pray to be admired. The Lord promises to hear and answer the prayers of his faithful children. He continually gives to all who seek him with their whole heart. A prayer journal and list are helpful to anyone who plans to spend much time in a healthy prayer life.

Meditation: Why did Jesus teach so much about prayer? What did his disciples see in the way that Jesus prayed that motivated them to ask for a lesson about prayer?

Prayer: Lord let me not pray like the hypocrites. Teach us how to fervently pray from a pure heart!

Closet Prayers
Matthew 6:6

"But thou, when thou prayest, enter into thy closet, and when thou hast shut thy door, pray to thy Father which is in secret; and thy Father which seeth in secret shall reward thee openly" (Matthew 6:6). Jesus chose to pray alone at times. His example shows us the great importance of a private prayer life. Closet prayers are an effective way for Christians to strengthen their resolve and personal relationship with Christ. First century Christians had busy prayer lives; they prayed often and were comforted and strengthened by a close communion with their Lord. No doubt, from time to time, there are secrets or private matters that Christians may wish only to share with a merciful, compassionate, and omniscient Father.

Meditation: Religious people in the first century loved to pray outdoors and in public places. Why did Jesus teach his disciples to pray privately, even in a closet?

Prayer: Lord, remind us daily of the life-altering power of prayer! Show us the better life through the power of frequent prayer!

Using Vain Repetitions
Matthew 6:7

"But when ye pray, use not vain repetitions, as the heathen do: for they think that they shall be heard for their much speaking" (Matthew 6:7). Repetitiveness in prayer is nonsensical, since the Lord already knows what we will say before it is said the first time. Both Jesus and Paul fervently prayed in times of great need. They repeated their requests to God to remove great burdens from their lives. Their prayers were never vain, but fervent and faithful, unlike the ritualistic and halfheartedly-repeated prayers of the heathens.

Meditation: Did the Lord answer the heathens' prayers despite their "vain repetitions"?

Prayer: Teach us, O Lord, to pray to thee with fervor!

Your Father Knows
Matthew 6:8; 1 Samuel 1:10-17

". . . for your Father knoweth what things you have need of, before ye ask him" (Matthew 6:8). The Lord knows every person's need, great or small. Being aware of this helps, comforts, and encourages every Christian approaching God's heavenly throne of grace and mercy. Rest assured, mankind has no greater need than that of spiritual salvation, but the power of prayer also extends to one's physical needs. Such

needs include, but are not limited to, physical health, family problems, and even job security.

Meditation: Since the Lord knows what we need before we ask him, should that change the way we approach Him?

Prayer: Lord, teach us to pray, understanding that thou already sees and knows all that we could bring before thee! May our prayers be like that of the righteous man, availing much.

Lord Teach Us to Pray
Matthew 6:9-12

"After this manner therefore pray ye: Our Father which art in heaven, Hallowed be thy name" (Matthew 6:9). What a blessing, to be able to address God as Father! The disciples had requested that Jesus teach them to pray, resulting in the model prayer. The prayer begins with an address to the Father, an endearment and salutation, then a plea for cleansing or forgiveness and a request to be delivered. Every word is couched in never ending gratitude. Many prayers have since been modeled after this very brief but powerful original template.

Meditation: Why was the prayer Jesus taught his disciples so brief?

Prayer: Lord, may our prayers be heartfelt and diligent. Help us to realize that practice is the key to improving our prayer lives!

Thy Kingdom Come
Matthew 6:9-13; Matthew 16:18-20;
1 Timothy 3:15

"Thy kingdom come, thy will be done . . ." (Matthew 6:10). Jesus stated in his prayer, *"Thy kingdom come."* The kingdom that Christ speaks of was near. Since God's kingdom and church are one and the same, then the church was also near to its establishment. After being prophesied about for centuries, Christ's church was finally promised by Jesus himself in Matthew 16:18, and later its evident establishment in Acts chapter two. It is referred to as Christ's "body" in Ephesians 1:22-23. Today, obedient believers are added to the church by the Lord himself (Acts 2:47). Doing the will of the Father is the only way dedicated disciples will have the hope of heaven someday (Matthew 7:21).

Meditation: When the apostle John writes that he was *"in the kingdom"* in Revelation 1:9, was he also implying that he had membership in Christ's body, the church?

Prayer: Lord, may we realize that your will is always done. Show us what it means to be a member of your body.

Week 8

Daily Bread

Matthew 6:9-15; Psalm 1

"Give us this day our daily bread" (Matthew 6:11). It is very helpful for Christians to remember to live one day at a time. It is critical that non-Christians and unchurched individuals be reminded of how short life really is and that today is the day for salvation! No one has the promise of tomorrow. With that being said, mankind needs more than physical nourishment to sustain life, for we are more than mere physical beings. The spiritual, inner person must be fed with spiritual food, so that he or she can *"grow in grace and in the knowledge of . . . Jesus Christ"* (2 Peter 3:18; 2 Corinthians 4:16).

Meditation: Does the Lord expect me to pray each day for my physical bread? How often should we expect to need spiritual sustenance?

Prayer: Lord, may we remember to give thanks daily. Help us to learn to enjoy with gratitude the abundant life you provide us with every day!

Forgive Us

Matthew 6:12; John 14:15; Luke 6:46; Matthew 7:21, 24-30

"And forgive us our debts, as we forgive our debtors" (Matthew 6:12). All are debtors! Mankind can never repay Jesus for what he did for every one of us by his

death on the cross. We all contributed to putting him there, and not one person is deserving of his salvation. Therefore, some have mistakenly believed that a Christian cannot now contribute anything towards his own soul's salvation, (obtaining salvation initially or by maintaining it), but this is not what the scriptures indicate at all. Each person is commanded to do his or her part, working out his or her own salvation, beginning with "hearing the word of God" in order to have faith (Romans 10:17). Notice that Jesus himself worked in the day, knowing that when night comes, *"no man can work"* (John 9:4). Remember, Jesus said that wise men are to build their houses on the Rock. To build a house takes much effort on a man's part. Although men do not earn their own salvation, they do build towards it!

Meditation: There are many commands for the New Testament Christian. Exactly which of those commands can a person ignore and still be pleasing to his Lord and Master?

Prayer: Lord, teach us to forgive others. Help us to forgive ourselves.

Deliver Us from Evil
Matthew 6:13; 2 Timothy 3:12

"And lead us not into temptation, but deliver us from evil:" (Matthew 6:13). Jesus' mission was to "seek and save the lost," and his Father, God, is the Great Deliverer. Through his Son, he has delivered his children from darkness into light. However, none are exempt from the trials and temptations that

46

challenge Christian service. The enemy is always on the prowl for another victory, but praise God, Jesus has gained the victory that overcomes the world!

Meditation: Could a Christian still pray The Lord's Prayer today? What is said to occur when one resists the devil? (See James 4:7.)

Prayer: Lord, teach us to resist the evil one at every turn. Help us in the fight against evil.

Forgive Others (70x7)
Matthew 6:14-15; Psalm 26

"For if ye forgive men their trespasses, your heavenly Father will also forgive you" (Matthew 6:14). When children of God desire forgiveness, then they should also show mercy to others. This is one of the basic tenants of Christianity. On one occasion, a disciple asked Jesus if he should forgive his brother seven times. In his mind, he perhaps thought that forgiving his brother seven times was a lot of mercy to extend to his brother. However, Jesus gives him a math equation that amounted to a much more substantial number, telling his disciple to forgive *"seventy times seven"* times (Matthew 18:21-22). The idea was not to forgive only a specified number of times (490), but rather that while our brother is asking for mercy that we continuously grant mercy.

Meditation: Is it possible to forgive someone and then un-forgive them? Is it possible to say the right words, and yet not feel the right feelings?

Prayer: Lord, teach us how to endlessly and truly forgive others. Help us to trust thee to forgive all thy children.

Fasting
Matthew 6:16-18; Mark 2:18-20

"Moreover when ye fast, be not, as the hypocrites . . ." (Matthew 6:16). Jesus' disciples were questioned one day about why they had not fasted, while John's disciples continued to observe the tradition. Jesus offered a good reason. While Jesus was still with them, his disciples had not felt the need to fast. However, he explained that after he returns to his Father in heaven, they will begin fasting once again. Although fasting is not a New Testament commandment, it is regulated, and some might argue, recommended, to us by the Lord. Jesus fasted for forty days while he was being tempted in the wilderness. Proper fasting is both a personal and private decision, though sometimes it can be encouraged and practiced congregationally. It serves to strengthen one's spiritual resolve, for in fasting, a person's body is denied the thing it is most focused on and cannot live without. Fasting also has some health benefits, but it should always be done prudently and with great caution.

Meditation: Why do you suppose some Christians feel commanded to fast today? Refer to the Bible for your answer. When did people of the Bible fast?

Prayer: Lord, teach us to deny ourselves and follow thee. Help us to know how best to follow thee from day to day.

True Wealth

Matthew 6:19-20; Luke 6:24; Matthew 6:24-34

"Lay not up for yourselves treasures upon earth, where moth and rust doth corrupt, and where thieves break through and steal: But lay up for yourselves treasures in heaven" (Matthew 6:19-20). Devoting all of one's time to the accumulation of earthly wealth will rob many of life's true riches. Missing the opportunities to lay up for ourselves treasures in heaven gives us a heart problem. Hearts will reside where our treasures hide. Wealth in and of itself is not evil, but the attitude of pursuing and accumulating earthly wealth while carelessly overlooking spiritual health prompted Jesus to observe how hard it is for a rich man to enter heaven (Matthew 19:23-24).

Meditation: Name at least three godly men in the Bible who were also rich.

Prayer: Lord, teach us to seek the things that are spiritual. Help us to accumulate heavenly treasures!

Are You Full of Light?

Matthew 6:22-23; 1 John 1:7-10; John 3:19-21; John 8:12; Revelation 3:10

"The light of the body is the eye: if therefore thine eye be single, thy whole body shall be full of light. But if thine eye be evil, thy whole body shall be full of darkness. If therefore the light that is in thee be darkness, how great is that darkness!" (Matthew 6:22-

23). The eye gathers light to be able to see clearly. Likewise, a person seeking spiritual enlightenment must embrace the path of light rather than that of darkness. Just as one should seek to be either hot or cold instead of lukewarm, one should not attempt to join light to darkness, creating merely dimness. Jesus, *"the light of the world,"* wants his followers to walk with him *"in the light."*

Meditation: What did Jesus mean about one's eye being "single"? According to Jesus, what causes the darkness to become "great"?

Prayer: Lord, may we choose the path of light. Teach us to be able to see clearly in a very dark world.

Week 9

Serving Two Masters
Matthew 6:24; Matthew 19:16-30

"No man can serve two masters: for either he will hate the one, and love the other; or else he will hold to the one, and despise the other. Ye cannot serve God and mammon" (Matthew 6:24). It may be said that no one can serve both God and (mammon) money. While this is indeed true, the term mammon has various meanings, including idolatrous worship. Love is about holding on to something without easily letting go. The Christian is instructed neither to love the world nor the things attached to it, but rather to love God with all of his heart, strength, soul, and mind. To do so is undeniable evidence that a Christian is committed to the Lord forever.

50

Meditation: How is serving two masters similar to what Jesus said in Revelation 3:14-22 to the church at Laodicea?

Prayer: Lord, teach us to be single-minded in our walk with thee! Grant us the wisdom we need to choose wisely!

Life Is More Than Food
Matthew 6:25

"Therefore I say unto you, Take no thought for your life, what ye shall eat, or what ye shall drink; nor yet for your body, what ye shall put on. Is not the life more than meat, and the body than raiment?" (Matthew 6:25). When people are too consumed with the needs of the body, they can eventually lose sight of the constant begging of their soul. Mankind's spirits long to be fed and clothed with the grace of God. Biblical Anorexia – the lack of consistent spiritual food – plagues our communities. However, within God's word mankind can find proper balance, nourishment and the abundant life.

Meditation: What are some danger signs for the Christian who may be getting off his spiritual track? What does the non-Christian need to understand about spiritual food before he/she becomes a child of God?

Prayer: Lord, thank you for the abundance of life. Teach us to seek those things that are above.

Our Father Feeds Birds
Matthew 6:26

"Behold the fowls of the air: for they sow not, neither do they reap, nor gather into barns; yet your heavenly Father feedeth them. Are ye not much better than they?" (Matthew 6:26). Jesus says that the fowls of the air do not plan ahead and store up for what they will eat, and yet God takes care of them. If God takes care of the smallest of his creatures, then we should not think he has forgotten about us. Our Father promises to take care of all of his children.

Meditation: How many sparrows would equal the value of a person's life? Do we worry too much about so many material things? Since the Lord promises to take care of our bodies' needs, then what does he do for our souls?

Prayer: Lord, let us not think of ourselves above that which we are, and may we know how to humble ourselves before thee.

Standing Taller
Matthew 6:27; 1 Timothy 4:8; 1 Corinthians 10:12

"Which of you by taking thought can add one cubit unto his stature?" (Matthew 6:27). Worry is no peacemaker! It is far better to accept the things we cannot change, no matter how much we worry about them. At times, there are things we can change! No special understanding or nerves of steel are needed

to advance spiritually. Fervent prayer and study can prepare us to make a difference or to know just when to give it all to God. *"Take therefore no thought for the morrow"* (Matthew 6:34). Be anxious (worry) for nothing and pray about everything! It will have us standing taller spiritually.

Meditation: What can change about ourselves? What are we guaranteed to be able to change about others?

Prayer: Lord, please give us the wisdom to know how to think. Teach us to set our minds on spiritual things.

What to Wear

Matthew 6:30; Hebrews 11:1, 6; Matthew 6:25

"Wherefore, if God so clothe the grass of the field, which today is, and tomorrow is cast into the oven, shall he not much more clothe you, O ye of little faith?" (Matthew 6:30). The Christian does not need to worry about having the necessities of life, including appropriate clothing. In addition, the Lord would have every one of His children clothed modestly. What the Christian chooses to wear is important because it indicates his or her inner purity. The Lord himself made clothes and gave them to Adam and Eve because the aprons they had designed and made for themselves were not adequate, for the Bible indicates they were still naked (Genesis 3:21). In ancient Hebrew times, *"the woman's clothing consisted of four garments. The inner garment – a closely fitted garment – was the most essential article of dress. It was without sleeves and reached only to the knees.*

Another of the garments reached to the wrist and ankles. It was in each case kept close to the body by a girdle, and the fold formed by the overlapping of the robe served as an inner pocket. A person wearing only the inner garment was described as naked" (Smiths Bible Dictionary).

Meditation: What was the difference in the clothes Adam and Eve made and the ones God tailored for them? Should we ever think about our clothing as it relates to our faith?

Prayer: Let us be aware that we are helped of thee. Dear Lord, teach us to seek thee with our whole heart!

He Knows Everything
Matthew 6:32; Romans 11:33-36

". . . for your heavenly Father knoweth that ye have need of all these things" (Matthew 6:32). God is aware of everything! He created us and knows every thought and desire of men's hearts. Though he knows beforehand what we will ask in prayer, he desires us to pray to him often. Paul wrote in 1 Thessalonians 5:17, "Pray without ceasing." Jesus told his disciples to address God as their Father, when they began to pray: "Our Father which art in heaven, hallowed be thy name" (Matthew 6:90). This same address to the Almighty or one like it will have God's faithful children speaking directly to him through his Son and our Savior, Jesus.

Meditation: Why do you suppose God wants us to pray when he already knows what we will say in that prayer?

Prayer: Our Father, we come before thee with thanksgiving. Teach us of thy ways and let us walk thy path.

First, Find the Kingdom
Matthew 6:33

"But seek ye first the kingdom of God, and his righteousness; and all these things shall be added unto you" (Matthew 6:33). Obviously, setting priorities is all about what is most important to us! We consider what we think about most and how we spend our time ordering tasks by first, second, and third priorities. Knowing the truth that sets men free and being faithful to God and to his kingdom – the church – should be at the top of everyone's list! Blessings abound for those who have their priorities properly aligned. The Lord promises to help us when we put him first in our lives.

Meditation: What steps could one take to do a better job devoting daily personal time to studying and prayer?

Prayer: Lord, help us to seek first thy righteousness. Teach us to arrange our priorities with you and the church in mind.

Week 10
Thinking of Tomorrow
Matthew 6:34; 1 Peter 5:8-11; James 4:13-17

"Take therefore no thought for the morrow: for the morrow shall take thought for the things of itself. Sufficient unto the day is the evil thereof" (Matthew 6:34). It is so easy to be concerned with things that haven't happened yet, and we tend to emphasize our future plans. As we set out to do our work, is God in our itinerary? Though our days are filled with new opportunities to do good, we know evil lurks in the shadows, eager to rob us of our happiness and devotion. If we allow evil to impregnate our hearts, it soon births bitterness, envy, and misery. There is a peace that can comfort the one who can stop worrying about tomorrow and take one day at a time.

Meditations: What are some ways to help someone resist Satan's advances more easily?

Prayer: O Lord, may we trust in thy power to save. Help us to be better prepared to fight the devil.

Judge Not
Matthew 7:1-2; John 7:24, 36-43

"Judge not, that ye be not judged. For with what judgment ye judge, ye shall be judged: and with what measure ye mete, it shall be measured to you again" (Matthew 7:1-2). Since how a person metes or measures out judgement is reciprocal, it is important

that we treat others as we want to be treated. Furthermore, is the Lord saying that no one can ever judge anything? While some may think so, this is actually not the meaning. Jesus is putting some conditions on the kind of judgment Christians are to use. He allows his faithful children to use righteous judgment, as they go about their busy lives for him. A Spiritual discernment is most needed in righteous judgment because it allows us to know right from wrong. And that knowledge needed to discern is found in Holy Scripture. Therefore, righteous judgment and spiritual discernment go hand in hand.

Meditation: Give two examples of when a Christian may judge. Give two examples of judgment not becoming of a Christian.

Prayer: Lord, let us not judge according to appearance. Teach us to be quick to hear but slow to speak.

Consider Your Problem First
Matthew 7:3-5; Mark 4:24-25; Luke 6:38-41

"And why beholdest thou the mote that is in thy brother's eye, but considerest not the beam that is in thine own eye? Or how wilt thou say to thy brother, Let me pull out the mote out of thine eye; and, behold, a beam is in thine own eye. Thou hypocrite, first cast out the beam out of thine own eye; and then shalt thou see clearly to cast out the mote out of thy brother's eye" (Matthew 7:3-5). One reason many give for leaving the path of righteousness and forsaking the Lord's

church (his people) is the discouragement they feel because of someone's hypocrisy. They have been bewildered by individuals espousing the name of Christ while living for the devil. Inspired scriptures admonish us to examine ourselves carefully; we may need to pull a beam from our own eye first! Anyone could point a finger at an obvious hypocrite, but shouldn't we also look around and see those who are trying hard to make a difference and live the right kind of life?

Meditation: Is the passage above teaching we should never correct a brother or sister who has a problem? What does it teach one should do first?

Prayer: Lord, teach us not to live a life of hypocrisy. Help us to be sure we are qualified before helping others.

Pearls before Swine
Matthew 7:6; 2 Peter 2:17-22

"Give not that which is holy unto the dogs, neither cast ye your pearls before swine, lest they trample them under their feet, and turn again and rend you" (Mathew 7:6). Some think that an opportunity should be given first to the person who has never heard the gospel before it is presented again and again to someone who has heard it many times and disregarded its loving invitation. It does seem some have had many opportunities to respond to the gospel's saving message, yet they refuse to obey. Are these people included in the Lord's definition of

"swine," or is he solely referring to those who blatantly scoff at his name?

Meditation: If there are individuals we are not supposed to teach or help, who are they? Should a Christian, a minister, or a shepherd ever give up on anyone?

Prayer: Lord, please teach us to love our neighbors as ourselves. Help us to manage ourselves and our spiritual lives well.

Ask, Seek, and Knock
Matthew 7:7-10; James 4:8

"Ask, and it shall be given you; seek, and ye shall find; knock, and it shall be opened unto you: For everyone that asketh receiveth; and he that seeketh findeth; and to him that knocketh it shall be opened" (Matthew 7:7-8). In each of the above activities listed, there are opportunities. When we involve ourselves in any of these spiritual activities, aren't we procuring a positive change in the outcome, beginning with a closer walk with the Savior? There is always something for us to do. There is always something more for us to contribute (Luke 6:46). Positive changes do not come without any cost or effort.

Meditation: What might be the very first step to a closer walk with the Lord? Second? Third?

Prayer: Dear Lord, let us draw closer unto thee. Let us be sure we know thee and are known of thee.

Asked for Bread; Got a Stone?

Matthew 7:9-11

"Or what man is there of you, whom if his son ask bread, will he give him a stone? Or if he asks a fish, will he give him a serpent? If ye then, being evil, know how to give good gifts unto your children, how much more shall your Father which is in heaven give good things to them that ask him?" (Matthew 7:9-11). Love always seeks to give the best gifts! Cruelty towards anyone, especially a family member, only brings heartache and ruin. We can learn how to be good by changing our hearts and attitudes toward others to be more like Jesus. Only then can we truly prosper and live the abundant and peaceful life that God has promised to all of his children. By the way, we can never out give God, because no one can ever out love him!

Meditation: What kind of things can the Father give us? Of those, what do you esteem the most important? Do you think he ever gives us anything we need but haven't asked for?

Prayer: Dear Lord, may we ask for those things that please thee. Help us to draw closer to thee each day!

The Golden Rule

Matthew 7:12

"Therefore all things whatsoever ye would that men should do to you, do ye even so to them: for this is the law and the prophets" (Matthew 7:12). Treating others with kindness is a true mark of Christianity

60

because it mirrors the Father's grace toward all his creation. No wonder it is called the golden rule. When God's children practice it, they become more like him. ("Each day I'll do a golden deed".) We can find the moorings of this New Testament principle long ago in the Old Covenant Law, as well as, in the Prophets.

Meditation: What blessings have you received as a result of practicing the golden rule?

Prayer: Lord, help us to treat others with kindness. Teach us to be busy in the Father's business.

Week 11
The Straight Gate
Matthew 7:13; Genesis 3:1-10; Luke 3:1-10

"Enter ye in at the strait gate: for wide is the gate, and broad is the way, that leadeth to destruction, and many there be which go in thereat" (Matthew 7:13). Jesus came to set the crooked things straight and smooth out the rough places (Luke 3:5). He promises every disciple an abundant life. Yet, sadly, not everyone has chosen to follow him. Many have traversed their own path, which might appear easy and popular at first and well-traveled for now, but later they discover that was not God's way. Instead, it is a dark path toward eternal ruin.

Similarly, in the Garden of Eden, two paths were available. They were represented by the tree of life and the tree of the knowledge of good and evil. Both trees were accessible in the garden, but only one offered eternal life. Unwisely, both Adam and Eve ate from the forbidden tree – the tree of the knowledge of good and evil – and were removed from their beautiful home. Don't be duped or seduced by the wrong way!

Meditation: What methods does Satan use to make the wrong way seem so right? What can people do if they want to uncover the truth about "the Way"?

Prayer: Lord, teach us to know the Way. Help us to choose wisely in this life.

The Narrow Way
Matthew 7:14; Matthew 11:28-33; Matthew 7:21-24

"Because strait is the gate, and narrow is the way, which leadeth unto life, and few there be that find it" (Matthew 7:14). Jesus said only a few will find the strait gate and narrow path that leads to eternal life. It will involve looking into God's word carefully, as if we were searching a road map to plan our next trip or to be certain we were on the right highway. David of long ago wrote in Psalm119 that God's word was a light to his path and a lamp to his feet. With this special light we can find God's highway and be sure we are on our way to heaven. His way might appear to be difficult, at first, and it will certainly have its challenges, but we are promised help along the way. In fact, Jesus said that his "yoke is easy" and his "burden is light".

Meditation: Why does the right way seem so difficult for many, while the wrong way seems so easy?

Prayer: Please open our eyes to see the truth about our way. Teach us to seek thee with our whole heart.

False Preachers
Matthew 7:15; Galatians 1:10; 1 John 5:1

"Beware of false prophets, which come to you in sheep's clothing but inwardly they are ravening wolves" (Matthew 7:15). Beware of false teachers! Some may genuinely believe their own teaching, but others are aware that they are seducing their followers and leading them astray. All the ravening wolves work for the prowling lion: Satan. These "false prophets" wear the garb of the righteous, yet they entertain evil and mislead the unaware. Surely, every vigilant child of God can be better prepared to fight the good fight. One way is by being keenly skillful in detecting false statements designed to cast the unprepared into a dark pit. Be diligent to know the truth; be an expert in the pure doctrine of Jesus Christ!

Meditation: Is it because of false preachers today that some never find the straight and narrow path?

Prayer: Let us find that straight and narrow way and choose to enter in. Teach us to be aware of the spiritual things that are so important.

Fruit Inspectors
Matthew 7:16; John 15:1-10

"Ye shall know them by their fruits. Do men gather grapes of thorns, or figs of thistles?" (Matthew 7:16). Good fruit is harvested from healthy and productive trees. Thorns and thistles cannot produce good fruit. Everyone will bear fruit, some good and some bad. So what kind of fruit tree are you? By the way, it's quite easy to get so busy inspecting the fruit of others that we forget to bear good fruit ourselves.

Meditation: Some fail to find the straight and narrow path because of false teachers. Some may never hear the gospel. What other reasons might prevent people from becoming Christians?

Prayer: Dear Lord, teach us to bear fruit for Thee. Help us to let our lights shine before others.

Good Tree = Good Fruit
Matthew 7:17-20; Luke 8:11

"Even so every good tree bringeth forth good fruit; but a corrupt tree bringeth forth evil fruit. A good tree cannot bring forth evil fruit, neither can a corrupt tree bring forth good fruit. Every tree that bringeth not forth good fruit is hewn down and cast into the fire. Wherefore by their fruits ye shall know them" (Matthew7:17-20). Good trees grow from good seed and the good seed is the word of God. Children of God bear fruit daily as they carry their Savior's cross. They deny themselves and suffer persecution for him.

At the same time, they bear the fruits of the Spirit. Then, when Christians share their faith and convert sinners from the error of their ways, the sin of the erring is removed and washed away. It gives reason for the angels in heaven to rejoice.

Meditation: Find the instance where the Lord told the gardener to cut down a fig tree. How many days had the fig tree stopped bearing fruit before the Lord said to cut it down? What does the story teach?

Prayer: Lord, help us to bear fruit consistently for thee. Teach us to know how to bear the fruit of the Spirit.

Is Everyone Going?
Matthew 7:21; 1 John 2:2

"Not everyone that saith unto me, Lord, Lord, shall enter into the kingdom of heaven; but he that doeth the will of my Father which is in heaven" (Matthew 7:21). Jesus says not everyone will go to heaven. He reveals that many religious people believe they know him! And though they might confess his name, they remain unknown to him. It is important that the Lord knows us. Though many may call on him in prayer and carry on various benevolent works in his name, it does not prove that a saving relationship exists. From the beginning, these same people never had the right kind of relationship with Him. The Lord said that the reason they will not enter heaven is because the will of "his Father" was not obeyed. Going to heaven is not a matter of good works alone, nor belief alone! Going to heaven is a matter of knowing the truth and

obeying God. Jesus knows all that truly know and love the Father. (See John 14:15 and Luke 6:46.)

Meditation: Does this statement by Jesus reveal that not everyone is going to heaven? If yes, then who is it that will enter in?

Prayer: Our Father, please teach us both to know and to obey thy will.

Lord! Lord!
Matthew 7:22; 1 John 3:7

"Many will say to me in that day Lord, Lord, have we not prophesied in thy name? And in thy name have cast out devils? and in thy name done many wonderful works?" (Matthew 7:22). Going to heaven is more than just being religious or feeling that we are close to the Lord because we have accomplished many good works in his name. Many will be denied access into the pearly gates, because they did not properly obey the will of the Father. It is possible to believe a lie for a lifetime about the Lord's commandments regarding salvation. Tragically, if we never learn the truth, we can be lost forever! We must know the actual truth that can release us from the burden of sin (John 8:32).

Meditation: Is Jesus saying here that it takes more than many good works to go to heaven? What else must be involved?

Prayer: Dear God, help us to be busy in your business. Let us draw close to thee with purity and the heart of a servant.

Week 12

Does He Know Me?

Matthew 7:23; 1 John 2:3-6; Galatians 4:9

"And then will I profess unto them, I never knew you: depart from me, ye that work iniquity" (Matthew 7:23). Jesus says the saved ones are those who keep His Father's will. His spiritual family represents a combined multitude, yet comparatively throughout history, the saved are fewer in number than the rest of the earth's population at any given time. While many religious people believe they have a personal relationship with Christ, everyone should search the scriptures and examine themselves to see if they are being saved or if they have been deceived by the enemy.

Meditation: When Elijah believed he was the only righteous one left in the land, what did the Lord remind him of? (Reference Romans 11:2-4.)

Prayer: Dear Father, teach us to always live for thee, no matter the circumstances.

Wise Man and Foolish Man
Matthew 7:24-27; Romans 10:17; Hebrews 11:6

"Therefore whosoever heareth these sayings of mine, and doeth them, I will liken him unto a wise man, which built his house upon a rock: And the rain descended, and the floods came, and the winds blew, and beat upon that house; and it fell not: for it was founded upon a rock. And every one that heareth these sayings of mine, and doeth them not, shall be likened unto a foolish man, which built his house upon the sand: And the rain descended, and the floods came, and winds blew, and beat upon that house; and it fell: and great was the fall of it" (Matthew 7:24-27). Building one's own house is difficult, which is why its recommended that most people hire a contractor. But we can't pay someone to build our spiritual houses for us. There are consequences and rewards for how people choose to live their lives. The results of our decisions will depend to a large degree on the foundation we have chosen. The best foundation can weather the most violent storms!

Meditations: In the children's song, "The Wise Man Built His House Upon the Rock," what happened to the foolish man's house? What do the rain, floods, and wind have in common in the song? Can you think of an Old Testament story where these were present? A New Testament one?

Prayer: Dear Father, teach us to search and find a solid foundation for our spiritual house.

I Will; Be Thou Clean
Matthew 8:3; 2 Peter 3:9; James 1:27

Jesus had compassion and healed many who suffered from diseases. He told a leprous man who had come to worship him, *"Be thou clean."* It was certainly within the will of the Lord for this man to be cleansed of his leprosy, but how much better is it for men to be cleansed from their sins? Some of the religious leaders in New Testament times heard Jesus teach that those who seemed religious outwardly would be better served to be clean inside and out. Imagine for a moment that people were plagued to wear all of their sins on the surface of their skin like leprosy. Would men be more eager to have their sins washed away if they could see them this way?

Meditation: If the Lord through prayer and his natural law can heal a person today from disease, can he not also heal a person from sin?

Prayer: Lord, help us to open our eyes to see thy will. O God, teach us to be clean both inside and out.

Great Faith
Matthew 8:10-13

"Verily I say unto you, I have not found so great faith, no, not in Israel" (Matthew 8:10). Even today, our Lord is looking for faith in people, and he points out that there are varying degrees of it. Learning that our faith can grow should encourage us. Since faith comes by hearing God's word, (Romans 10:17), we can hear

it and use it more as we live our lives. Jesus complimented the centurion's faith and then compared it to the lesser faith of all those in Israel.

Meditation: What made this man's faith so great? Was it something he said or did or both? Can a person have that kind of faith today?

Prayer: Lord, O God, teach us to increase our faith.

Foxes Have Holes

Matthew 8:20; Proverbs 23:1-5; James 5:1-6

". . . The foxes have holes, and the birds of the air have nests; but the Son of man hath not where to lay his head" (Matthew 8:20). Jesus did not own real-estate; he was just passing through. He never had a place he could call his own, though all of the earth is his and his Father's. Why would he ever want earthly riches when he was given a name above all names and exalted to the highest position in heaven at the right hand of God? He knew his forever home was not of this world. His life was similar in some ways to Jacob's, whose pillow was a stone. Jesus shared with his followers that God would lead and take care of them. Jesus wants all of his future disciples to count the cost of discipleship and realize the dangers and deceitfulness of riches. The goal is not to become too comfortable in this life; if we do, we may forfeit our next one.

Meditation: Since the world is not our forever home, is it acceptable to make plans to purchase homes and property? If so, when might the Lord find it unacceptable?

Prayer: O God, teach us to adjust our attitudes properly, especially when it concerns money.

Dead Bury the Dead
Matthew 8:22; Mark 2:14; Luke 9: 57-62

". . . Follow me; and let the dead bury their dead" (Matthew 8:22). Jesus often used parallelisms to teach. Here he offers a comparison showing that while some are going about their busy lives, they have no interest in spiritual things, so he describes them as dead. On the surface, the Lord's statement appears cold and unfeeling, yet no one was more compassionate toward others than Jesus. So here, he shows that discipleship calls us to a higher standard. He declares that there will always be those who are uninterested in Christianity, indifferent to the faithful follower of Jesus, and sometimes, even enemies of the cross of Christ.

Meditation: What kind of things today might hinder a Christian from enjoying a closer walk with the Lord?

Prayer: Lord, may we follow thee with our whole hearts.

Why Are You Afraid?
Matthew 8:23-27; James 2:14-26; Hebrews 11:6; Romans 10:17

". . . Why are ye fearful, O ye of little faith?" (Matthew 8:26). Degrees of faith are mentioned throughout the sacred text. Here, Jesus explains that fear was the reason for their diminished faith. When the great squalls had engulfed their ship on this occasion, Jesus – the great peacemaker – was sleeping. He was and is our perfect example of peace, perfect peace!

Meditation: If being fearful is being full of fear, and being doubtful is being full of doubt, what is it to be faithful?

Prayer: Lord, teach us to build up our faith upon thy wonderful promises!

Week 13
Arise and Walk
Matthew 9:5; Acts 4:1-10

"For whether is easier, to say, Thy sins be forgiven thee; or to say, Arise, and walk?" (Matthew 9:5). Wisely, Jesus ties together both physical and spiritual healing. These words spoken by our Lord are demonstrated today by each obedient disciple of Christ. He or she is first to arise from the water of baptism (Acts 22:16) with all sins being forgiven, and then to walk daily in the light of the glorious Gospel of Jesus Christ (John 1:7).

Meditation: Is it possible for us to know which of the two statements was easier for Jesus to say?

Prayer: Lord, let us walk closer to thee each day.

The Great Physician
Matthew 9:12; Ecclesiastes 12:13

"... *They that be whole need not a physician, but they that are sick*" (Matthew 9:12). Jesus came to seek and save the lost. He described those who had sin as being sick, while describing those who had been reborn as spiritually healthy. He told Nicodemus to be born again (John 3:3). This rebirth involves proper faith as well as baptism for the remission of sins. (See Mark 16:16.)

Meditation: What did Jesus mean when He said, "*They that be whole*" (Matthew 9:12)?

Prayer: Lord, please heal our sin sickness!

I Will Have Mercy?
Matthew 9:13

"*But go ye and learn what that meaneth, I will have mercy, and not sacrifice: for I am not come to call the righteous, but sinners to repentance*" (Matthew 9:13). Jesus said he wanted mercy and not sacrifice, but what exactly does that mean? If we are not sure then we too should "go and learn" servanthood, one of those things we should practice in our daily lives.

Though it involves sacrifice, mercy is also a path of healing through humility and loving others. Everyone should learn that grace saves us through repentance (Luke 13:3; Acts 2:38). It is fundamental to Christianity; without it we cannot be saved.

Meditation: Do some religious people today spend more time focused on sacrifice than on mercy?

Prayer: Dear Father, please forgive us of all our sins today!

The Days Will Come
Matthew 9:15

"Can the children of the bridechamber mourn, as long as the bridegroom is with them? But the days will come, when the bridegroom shall be taken from them and then shall they fast" (Matthew 9:15). Jesus states that while he was on earth and with his disciples, they would have little reason to fast because they experienced joy by being in his presence daily. However, the time to fast would come later. Christians might fast today in order to procure a closer walk with the Lord. In the battle against sin, some could very well benefit from fasting, ultimately avoiding continuation of sin that causes separation from God in eternity. (See Romans 6:1-3.)

Meditation: Does this passage teach that all Christians are commanded to fast today until Jesus returns?

Prayer: Dear Father, grant us a closer walk with thee.

New Wine and New Bottles
Matthew 9:17

"*Neither do men put new wine into old bottles: else the bottles break, and the wine runneth out, and bottles perish: but they put new wine into new bottles, and both are preserved*" (Matthew 9:17). Both the old and new covenants are under discussion. It was prevalent in the first century to mix the two laws, keeping some of the old while abiding in some of the new. This still happens today. For example, instruments are being used in contemporary worship services, a practice some point to in the Old Law, though it is not authorized anywhere in the New Testament. Jesus is teaching that the Old Law has been fulfilled, thus ending its observances. It is the New Testament that Christians should follow today. Perhaps another idea here from Christ's teaching is that Christians who are faithful "unto death" shall receive new bodies for their renewed spirits. (See 1 Corinthians 15).

Meditation: What other passages teach that the Old Law or Old Testament was fulfilled?

Prayer: Lord, let us not do anything to hurt or diminish our righteous influencing of others.

The Sabbath
Mark 2:25-28

". . . *The Sabbath was made for man, not man for the Sabbath*" (Mark 2:27). It is quite common today for men to get caught up in the ceremonial or traditional parts of their religion. But pure religion is certainly an "obey from the heart" kind of religion. The Old Sabbath was a day of rest for the Jews and not binding on Christians today, but there is coming a Sabbath for all who live righteously. It is described in scripture as being for all who will inhabit heaven. Worship for Christians today is to be on Sunday, the first day of the week. An example of Christian observance in worship on this day is clearly seen in Acts 20:7. This day's worship activities should be held in high regard as was the Sabbath Day in the Old Testament.

Meditation: Why is heaven a type of Sabbath for the people of God who will be judged worthy?

Prayer: Dear God, teach us to always be ready for Christ's return!

A Divided House
Mark 3:22-30

"And if a house be divided against itself, that house cannot stand" (Mark 3:25). The attempt to hold on to Christ while at the same time abiding in the world and enjoying the pleasures of sin will not give us the results we want. True wealth and success result from a Christ-centered life. Christians are told that it simply isn't possible to serve God and mammon—that is things and money. We must choose a life with God as our Master and Christ as our Savior if we wish to have the promise of eternal life.

Meditation: What does the scripture reveal about a "divided" house?

Prayer: Lord, teach us how to have unity at home.

Week 14
So Many Blessings!
Luke 6:38; 1 Corinthians 16:1-2

"Give, and it shall be given unto you; good measure, pressed down, and shaken together, and running over, shall men give into your bosom. For with the same measure that ye mete withal it shall be measured to you again" (Luke 6:38). Mercy is often shown and measured by our giving. Jesus is teaching the principle of reaping what we sow. He says that you will receive "with the same measure" that you give. Giving to those in need shows compassion and love, and treating our neighbors as ourselves is Christ-like. Christian behavior is always rewarded favorably. In the text above, physical things – or goods – are discussed; however, this principle applies to spiritual labor as well, such as is seen in the Lord's Prayer: *"Forgive us our debts, as we forgive our debtors."* The principle of reaping what we sow is applied to sin as well as to judgments (Matthew 7:1).

Meditation: The Christian is commanded to give as an activity of worship. Money is collected each Lord's Day and becomes part of the common treasury. Could it be beneficial to increase our weekly contribution with the sole purpose of receiving a return on our investment from the Lord?

Prayer: Lord, teach us how to give cheerfully!

Blind Leading the Blind
Luke 6:39-42

". . . Can the blind lead the blind? Shall they not both fall into the ditch?" (Luke 6:39). Christ uses an obvious absurdity to express a spiritual sense: it is foolish for the blind to attempt to lead the blind or for the blind to follow the blind. Just a handful of people can walk a tight rope blindfolded. Very few would ever want to try it! Why, then, are there so many risk takers when it comes to walking the straight and narrow path? It is far better to keep our eyes wide open as we follow Jesus and look at the truth revealed to us in the scriptures. It will surely help us to have solid footing, prevent many of life's pitfalls, and lead others along a better path. True faith is not blind faith, but rather a faith built on all the promises of God. (See Hebrews 11:1.)

Meditation: Is it possible today for one to follow a spiritual leader who is blind to the truth? How could one free himself of the impending danger of falling?

Prayer: Lord, teach us to obey you and not man.

More about Jesus
Luke 6:40

"The disciple is not above his master: but everyone that is perfect shall be as his master" (Luke 6:40). When we strive for perfection, we become more and more like our Father. When we are more like God, we are also more like our Savior as well (Matthew 5:48). Growing in grace and knowledge is a process. (See Galatians 3:27; Romans 12:2.)

Meditation: What do we need to do to become more like Jesus and to know what he would do in every circumstance? Would it help to study more about him and his life?

Prayer: Dear Father, let us be more like Jesus.

Doing What Jesus Says
Luke 6:46

"And why call ye me, Lord, Lord, and do not the things which I say?" (Luke 6:46). Here is one of the Lord's most telling statements, mainly because it closely resembles our religious environment today. It highlights the individual who thinks he knows the Lord and confesses the Lord's name among men, yet he is never actually pleasing to the Lord. Being *"in Christ"* is absolutely necessary for one to be saved from his sins and become a member of the Lord's body, the church. Only obedient individuals that have been truly saved and adopted into God's family can

justifiably call him their Lord and Savior. (See Galatians 3:27; Romans 6:3-4; and Malachi 1:6.)

Meditation: Is it possible for a person to think he or she is saved, and yet not be? How could one best avoid this problem?

Prayer: Lord, teach us to truly know thee!

The Gospel Is Preached
Luke 7:22-29

". . . Go your way, and tell John what things ye have seen and heard; how that the blind see, the lame walk, the lepers are cleansed, the deaf hear, the dead are raised, to the poor the gospel is preached" (Luke 7:22). Answered prayers are to a Christian like gold is to a miner: highly valuable. So often we need assurance that God is working in our lives. But notice that the rich are not mentioned above. They need salvation, too, but the Lord described them as having placed too much trust in their possessions to devote their lives in a meaningful way for their Savior.

Meditation: Since these kinds of miracles are not being performed any longer, how can one truly come to know the Lord and recognize him as Master?

Prayer: Lord, as we study, show us the truth about Jesus.

He Is Greater Than John
Matthew 16:18; Matthew 28:19-20; Acts 2:38-47

"For I say unto you, Among those that are born of women there is not a greater prophet than John the Baptist: but he that is least in the kingdom of God is greater than he" (Luke 7:28). Though John was a prophet and a faithful servant, he was executed by Herod before he could ever become a member of the Lord's promised institution, the church. John was aware that the establishment of the Lord's church was imminent; he also knew that Christ must be the head of his body: the church, and that he must take a lesser role to that of his Savior. John said, "He must increase, but I must decrease" (John 3:30).

Meditation: What would John the Baptizer have had to do to become a member of Christ's church?

Prayer: Lord, let us pay attention to your will, O God.

You Have not Danced
Luke 7:31-35

"They are like unto children sitting in the marketplace, and calling one to another, and saying, We have piped unto you, and ye have not danced; we have mourned to you, and ye have not wept" (Luke 7:32). Children of God are a peculiar people and will rarely behave as the world does. Christ-like individuals know that they are like Jesus and live in this world, but certainly they cannot participate in every activity. Sin has its pleasures, but so does Christianity! Followers of

Christ who desire to walk in the footsteps of Jesus see that the benefits of their commitments are eternal instead of temporary in nature. No doubt, unchurched friends of Christians at times become ashamed or uncomfortable with the Bible's position about proper behavior. The uneasiness that some may experience in the company of a child of light may impress on their minds their own need for salvation by means of a closer walk with the Savior.

Meditation: Why had the children, mentioned above, not danced when the music for dancing was being played?

Prayer: Lord, let us avoid the world and be Christ-like.

Week 15
Loving Him More
Luke 7:41-43

"And when they had nothing to pay, he frankly forgave them both. Tell me therefore, which of them will love most?" (Luke7:42). Through the sacrifice of Jesus upon his cross, his disciples today can have the remarkable blessing and gift of a clean heart and conscience. The Christian now must always carry, not sit on, his cross. He is free from sin but not from duty. He or she must always contribute to his or her own salvation. This is how one demonstrates love for God.

Meditation: How does Jesus connect love with forgiveness?

Prayer: Lord, teach us to love thee more each day.

Is It Ever Okay to Judge?
Luke 7:40-50

"*. . . Thou hast rightly judged*" (Luke 7:43). Some demand that Christians should never judge others. If that were true, why then did Jesus say that Simon had "judged rightly"? Is it not because Christians would be commanded to judge righteously? In other words, we may use the judgments that have already been provided to us within the scriptures. In the teaching moment that Jesus shares with Simon, Jesus asks Simon to make a judgment by choosing which person in his example had more love. Our Savior, being the perfect teacher, gives us an excellent example here of making a proper or right judgement; furthermore, he shows us the attitude we should have when judging.

Meditation: Are there times when we should not judge? Give examples. What can we learn from Jesus' response that Simon had judged righteously?

Prayer: Lord, help us to open our eyes to see thy will. O God, teach us to know how to judge righteously.

Be Born Again!

John 3:1-9

"... Verily, Verily, I say unto thee, Except a man be born again, he cannot see the kingdom of God" (John 3:3). Jesus said a person must be born of water and the Spirit. Some have argued that by using "water," Jesus meant the water associated in one's natural birth. Yet, Jesus used the term of an adult when he said, "Except a **man**" be born again. Notice to be "born again" takes both "water and Spirit". One who anticipates entry into heaven must have proper faith and be immersed into Jesus Christ for the remission of sins. Only then can he be born again. After his conversion, he is to continue to trust and obey God until his appointment with death and then the judgement (Hebrews 9:27; Revelation 2:10).

Denominations are generally religions of contradiction, teaching a variety of opposing beliefs about many things, but especially about how a person is to be born again with immersion. Although Jesus was referring to baptism he didn't use that word with Nicodemus. When a person looks further in scripture; he sees that water is mentioned again and again in association with baptism (immersion) and salvation. An example is in this chapter in verse 23. Here, John is baptizing in a place called "Aenon" because there was "much" water there. If baptism isn't an immersion, then there would have been little reason to choose that location. Later, on the Day of Pentecost in Acts 2:38, believers would be baptized in "water and the Spirit" for the remission of their sins.

Meditation: Did Nicodemus' question reveal that he did not understand about such things? What did he know about Jesus? Since he was a Jewish leader, what would he have been taught as a child? Investigate requirements for salvation by five denominations.

Prayer: Lord, help us to open our eyes to see thy will, O God! Help us to understand the truth about baptism and how we are saved.

Teachers Should Know
John 3:10-15

"Art thou a master of Israel, and knowest not these things?" (John 3:10). Nicodemus, a supposed expert of the Old Law, did not know the answer to a simple question regarding salvation. If one were to inquire with ten different religions today, he might receive various answers to the same soul- saving question or possibly no answer at all. Receiving different answers to our most sincere religious questions is confusing, at best. And since our heavenly Father says he is not the author of confusion, then who is?

Meditation: Isn't it confusing when one receives different answers to the same question? Did Jesus or any of the eight named authors of the New Testament ever contradict one another?

Prayer: Lord, teach us to know thy true teachings.

The Golden Text
John 3:16-18

"For God so loved the world, that he gave his only begotten Son, that whosoever believeth in him should not perish but have everlasting life" (John 3:16). This verse of scripture is one of the world's most familiar Bible passages, and yet it may be the most misinterpreted as well. The context of this verse does not support that of a "belief only" salvation. The meaning here is much deeper and richer than can be gathered through a single glance of the text. The verses before and after this one should be read and studied in order to obtain a more accurate interpretation of the text. (John 3:10-20).

Meditation: Does the Bible distinguish between belief "in" and belief "on" Christ?

Prayer: Lord, teach us to truly believe in the Truth.

Light Has Come
John 3:19

"Light is come into the world, and men loved darkness rather than light, because their deeds were evil" (John 3:19). Sinners often enjoy one another's company. They can be quite embarrassed at times to be in the company of Christians, who refuse to participate in any lewd activities. Armed with this knowledge, Christians today have an advantage when reaching

out to the lost and evangelizing those of their community.

Meditation: Why is it that those who live a worldly lifestyle think it strange that you do not share that lifestyle with them?

Prayer: Lord, may our love for the fellowship of the righteous grow exponentially greater than our love for the company of sinners!

Everlasting Water
John 4:13-14

". . . *Whosoever drinketh of this water shall thirst again: But whosoever drinketh of the water that I shall give him shall never thirst*" (John 4:14). Jesus' life and death prove that men cannot live by bread alone. Everyone needs spiritual meat. Obviously, physical and spiritual food are different. One of the major differences is the quality and quantity of life that each produces. For example, H_2O will give us what is needful for the body, but spiritual water is for our souls. Physical water may quench one's thirst down a dusty road for a while, but the water Jesus describes leads us on God's spiritual highway and gets us to heaven for eternity!

Meditation: How does one actually drink of spiritual water? Is it also the fountain of youth?

Prayer: Lord, help us to hunger and thirst after righteousness.

Week 16

Where to Worship
John 4:21

". . . the hour cometh, when ye shall neither in this mountain, nor yet at Jerusalem, worship the Father" (John 4:21). It would be difficult if all Christians were required to travel to present day Jerusalem and offer their worship there. The New Testament supports Christian worship in any city. Sunday services can be conducted anywhere. Having them in a church building is extremely convenient, but not absolutely necessary. The Sermon on the Mount was on a mountain, and many such authentic services – modern and past – have been conducted outside. The "when" and "how" is much more important than the "where" (John 4:20-26).

Meditation: Does it matter where we worship? Must we have a church building?

Prayer: Lord, let us worship thee acceptably.

How to Worship
John 4:24

"God is a Spirit: and they that worship him must worship him in spirit and in truth" (John 4:24). The term "must" in the Lord's statement regarding worship makes it imperative. True worship is commanded of all of God's children. Sunday worship has five activities: giving, the Lord's Supper, acapella singing, prayer, and teaching. In 1 Corinthians 16:1-2, we find that our giving to God is a matter of worship that is observed "every first day of the week" (ERV), with four more activities of worship each Lord's Day. Our worship should be meaningful and respectful, but it must also observe the pattern that God has outlined in his word. (See 1 Corinthians 16:1-2; Acts 20:7; Ephesians 5:19; Luke 18:1; and 1 Timothy 4:2).

Meditation: What is worshipping in spirit all about? Worshipping in truth?

Prayer: Lord, may we all worship thee in spirit and in truth!

Finishing His Work
John 4:31-34

". . . *My meat is to do the will of him that sent me, and to finish his work*" (John 4:34). Jesus was accomplishing his Father's work for him at the tender age of twelve years. Around the age of thirty, he began his ministry. Only three years later, while dying on the cross for all of humanity, he uttered, "It is finished," and then gave his spirit back to God. His death put the finishing touches on the Old Covenant evidenced in the tearing of the veil of the temple. (John 19:30; Matthew 27:51; Mark 15:38; Luke 23:45). Its separation into two pieces marked the arrival of a New Covenant between the Lord and his people. Incidentally, the veil's tensile strength was similar to steel, yet was found torn uniformly in two from top to bottom. It has been conjectured that it would have taken several horse drawn chariots to have pulled it apart!

Meditation: What did the tearing of the veil represent? When men first saw that the veil was in two pieces, how do you think they reacted? What might this reveal about any teaching today that threatens Christ's doctrine?

Prayer: Lord, may we tear down every high thing that may oppose thee!

A White Harvest
John 4:35-38

"Say not ye, There are yet four months, and then cometh harvest? Behold, I say unto you, Lift up your eyes, and look on the fields; for they are white already to harvest" (John 4:35). It is apparent that Jesus can see things that are invisible to us. He is aware of what people have in their minds and hearts. We may not know for sure whether the statement "fields of white" was a reference to cotton or some other white produce, or if Jesus was merely using the idea to describe the white robes of future Christians. We can know that in scripture, white represents purity. Sins are washed away today by the blood of the lamb. This happens during an immersion in water called baptism. Baptism represents a burial with Christ according to Romans 6:3-4.

Meditation: Does the statement by Jesus in John 4:35 reveal that more people are ready to obey the gospel than we may realize? How does one plant the seed of the gospel?

Prayer: Lord, may we also see those who are ready or who only need the slightest encouragement to obey the gospel of Jesus Christ!

Give Me a Sign
John 4:46-54

"Except ye see signs and wonders, ye will not believe" (John 4:48). John is writing about the second miracle Jesus performed after going into Galilee (John 4:54). First century believers were criticized when Jesus noticed their unbelief. According to the Hebrew writer, faith is the evidence of things not seen (Hebrews 11:1). Sadly, Christians today stumble after the same pattern of small faith when they seek after supernatural evidence, forsaking the very definition of faith. Trusting in a living God means believing in someone that we don't readily see with our physical eyes or measure with any of our five senses. For example, we have not actually seen Jesus or heard him speak, yet faith is evident and has substance. Jesus revealed the measurability of faith with statements like "O ye of little faith" and "great is thy faith." Having great faith today does not mean embracing now those things that were told to have cessation, like speaking in tongues or performing miracles; faith comes merely by the hearing of God's word (Romans 10:17). Thus faith today is shown by its works, which are acts of love.

Meditation: Jesus raised Lazarus from the dead after he had been four days in the tomb. On a practical note, if miracles like that are still being performed today, wouldn't such an event be newsworthy?

Prayer: Lord, teach us to rightly divide thy words.

Sin No More
John 5:1-16

"Behold, thou art made whole: sin no more, lest a worse thing come unto thee" (John 5:14). The man Jesus heals here had been sick for thirty-eight years. Jesus says to him that if he doesn't stop the practice of sin, something worse could come to him. Often, sin is the culprit for our many misfortunes. It robs us of our happiness, our health, our contentment, and ultimately, our souls. To be healed of our sin and made whole by the Great Physician is the ultimate blessing.

Meditation: What *"worse thing"* could Jesus have had in mind concerning this man?

Prayer: Lord, teach us to get up from our beds of sin and follow thee, walking in the light all the while.

My Father Is Working
John 5:17

"My Father worketh hitherto, and I work" (John 5:17). The Father, the Son, and the Holy Spirit all work together to provide man his precious gift of salvation. Once people find and receive salvation, there is more spiritual work to be done. It involves fighting the good fight of faith and finishing the course. It is about our continuing commitment, keeping the faith, and walking in the light alongside the Savior. Incidentally, this statement in John was made about labor done on the Sabbath Day. When the Christian age began, the prohibition of work on each Sabbath Day, which was commanded under the Law of Moses, ended.

Meditation: If the Lord wants individuals to follow Him, then what should the Christian's spiritual work ethic look like? Shouldn't people be willing to contribute to their own salvation? Consider the following: *". . . work out your own salvation with fear and trembling"* (Philippians 2:12). How many good works does it take to get to heaven?

Prayer: Lord, teach us to obey thy will and contribute to our own salvation!

Week 17
Follow the Leader
John 5:19-27

". . . *The Son can do nothing of himself, but what he seeth the Father do: for what things soever he doeth, these also doeth the son likewise*" (John 5:19). Jesus was a faithful and obedient Son. He communicated to the lost the special message of love that his Father had prepared for mankind whether that message took the form of words or deeds. Unlike the animal sacrifices of yesteryear, Jesus was the perfect sacrifice. He was that sacrificial lamb that taketh away the sins of the world. There are many sacrifices that Christians must make today, too, as they follow the leader.

Meditation: Shouldn't it profit the Christian today to follow in the steps of Christ? What will the world around us see when this happens?

Prayer: Lord, teach us to let our lights so shine to others!

The Hour Is Coming
Matthew 24:36; Matthew 7:21

". . . *the hour is coming, in the which all that are in the graves shall hear his voice, And shall come forth; they that have done good, unto the resurrection of life; and they that have done evil, unto the resurrection of damnation*" (John 5:28-29). There has already been a time chosen for the Lord's return, although man is unaware of the day or hour of it. Therefore, it behooves every one of us to be ready each day to face our Lord unannounced. When the last hour does come there will be a resurrection of both the righteous and the unrighteous.

Meditation: Does the Bible indicate whom will rise first? What does the Bible say about new bodies for the righteous?

Prayer: Lord, may we see thy grand purpose for our individual lives!

Burning and Shining
John 5:30-36

"I can of mine own self do nothing: as I hear, I judge: and my judgment is just; because I seek not mine own will, but the will of the Father which hath sent me" (John 5:30). Jesus said that John the Baptizer was a burning and shining lamp who had identified him as the "Lamb of God" that should take away the sins of the world. But Jesus had a greater witness than that of John, for his was the work that the Father had sent him to do. When Jesus was only twelve –years-old, he was already about his Father's business. Later, he testified during his three-year-ministry that he had come to seek and save the lost!

Meditation: Search the scriptures for the names of Timothy's mother and grandmother. Both influenced his faith in God while he was a youth.

Prayer: Lord, teach us to learn how to begin serving thee.

Haven't Seen His Shape
Romans 10:17; John 17:17

"And the Father himself, which hath sent me, hath borne witness of me. Ye have neither heard his voice at any time, nor seen his shape. And ye have not his word abiding in you." (John 5:37-38). Today, though we haven't seen God's exterior shape or heard his voice speaking to us, we can have his word living inside of us. We can hear his words, build our faith, and keep his commandments. Jesus had told his followers that when they looked at him that they were also looking at his Father. We can observe the Father with eyes of faith today; this kind of faith positively shapes our lives as well as the lives of others.

Meditation: How do people benefit when God's word dwells in them? How exactly does the Word dwell within us?

Prayer: Lord, teach us to allow thy words to dwell always within us!

Search the Scriptures
1 Peter 3:18; 2 Timothy 2:15; Matthew 4:4

"Search the scriptures; for in them ye think ye have eternal life: and they are they which testify of me" (John 5:39). With a closer examination of scripture and with open ears and hearts, searchers can

discover the truth and claim for themselves eternal life. Armed with zeal and renewed with knowledge, we are able to discern between good and evil, truth and error. The noble Bereans did this daily in Acts 17 and were complimented for it. A diet rich in grace and knowledge will help each follower of Christ to grow up well-edified in the Spirit.

Meditation: If Bible study is similar to eating food, then what might happen to the Christian who forgets to study regularly?

Prayer: Lord, give us a desire to know the scriptures that can make us wise unto salvation.

Come to Jesus
Matthew 11:28-30

"And ye will not come to me, that ye might have life" (John 5:40). Many reject the Lord's invitation to come to Him. It is a matter of life and death not to do so. Not only does the Lord promise to give life, but he offers it in abundance! He has invited every person to come to him by taking up his cross daily. He says that everyone has a burden of sin that he cannot successfully carry alone. That is why he said for us to take his yoke upon us and to learn of him.

Meditation: Why do so many refuse the Lord's invitation?

Prayer: Lord, help us to open our eyes to see thy will. O God! Let us draw nigh to Jesus with every opportunity we receive!

Having Honor
John 5:41

"I receive not honor from men" (John 5:41). Devoted disciples of Christ long for their Lord's approval. For them, it is about a sincere faith and unfeigned righteousness. Unfortunately, some seek only the honor that comes from man's recognition while being at the same time uninterested in seeking God's grace and favor. But we can have both!

Meditation: How can we have God's grace and favor and man's recognition simultaneously?

Prayer: Lord, may we seek thy grace and favor in everything we do!

Week 18

The Love of God
John 5:42

"But I know you, that ye have not the love of God in you" (John 5:42). Jesus knows us and is deeply aware of what is in our hearts. A heart filled with love for God never escapes the Lord's notice and will always demonstrate character to those around it. Jesus explained, *"By this all men will know you are my disciples."* The obvious and primary way that Christians know if someone loves God is by his or her loyal obedience to God's commandments. (See Luke 6:46; John 14:15; 1 John 2:1-5.)

Meditation: Could someone's dress or language ever provide a clue as to how spiritual that person is or if that person is truly a Disciple of Christ?

Prayer: Lord, teach us to love and trust Thee more!

Accusations
John 5:45-47

"Do not think that I will accuse you to the Father: there is one that accuseth you, even Moses, in whom ye trust" (John 5:45). The word of God will judge us on the last day (John 12:48). But how could Moses accuse them when he had been dead for centuries? Moses is mentioned in the text because the Jews had a law from God given to them through Moses. Because of this, they would be judged on the last day at the great judgement by the Old Law's teachings. However, those who lived after the cross would be judged by the law of Christ, the teachings of the New Testament.

Meditation: Why had the Jews put their trust in Moses?

Prayer: Lord, help us to live up to thy expectations. O God, teach us to examine our hearts to be sure we have proper faith.

Seeking Spiritual Food
John 6:1-26

"Ye seek me, not because ye saw the miracles, but because ye did eat of the loaves, and were filled" (John 6:26). Here is an example of people living by bread alone (Matthew 4:4). It is all too easy for us to get so caught up in our "every day work" world that we lose sight of the true meaning of life. (See John 5:27; Matthew 6:33.)

Meditation: What does the Lord promise to all of those that first seek him and his kingdom?

Prayer: Lord, help us to examine thy will for our lives. O God, teach us to long for spiritual food!

Belief, a Work of God
John 6:29

"This is the work of God that ye believe on him whom he hath sent" (John 6:29). Clearly, believing in Jesus is a work of God, alongside confession, repentance, and baptism. All of these are absolutely necessary for one to be considered as saved (Acts 2:38, 47). In fact, Jesus made all these prerequisites for salvation as he spoke of them throughout the four Gospels. Who could deny that one must believe in Jesus after reading John 3:16, probably one of the most recognized verses of New Testament scripture? Likewise, who could deemphasize baptism when Jesus was so clear about it in Mark 16:16?

Meditation: Since the Lord told his followers what they must do in order to be saved, could they disregard any of those things and still be pleasing to their Master? Why or why not?

Prayer: Lord, help us to accomplish all thy will. O God, teach us to love thee more!

Bread of Life
John 6:35

"I am the bread of Life: he that cometh to me shall never hunger; and he that believeth on me shall never thirst" (John 6:35). Creating a spiritual diet consisting of study and prayer is often a challenge. Finding the time in our busy schedules is difficult, but the rewards are out of this world. Begin today to find at least five minutes daily to consistently spend in devotion to God.

Meditation: Are coming to Jesus and believing on Jesus two different things? Are the ideas of spiritually eating and drinking two different things? Is someone misled who believes in a "belief only" salvation? (See James 2:19.)

Prayer: Lord, teach us to fill ourselves with thy goodness!

My Words are Spiritual
John 6:63

". . . the words I speak unto you, they are spirit, and they are life" (John 6:63). The wonderful words of life that proceeded from the mouth of our Lord are certainly words to live by. The same cannot be said of all the words expressed by the philosophers and talented, educated, and popular authors or professors, enlighteners or supposed "experts." This should especially apply to matters of religion and salvation. Besides, there is no greater intelligence in anything than in the one that made everything: our Lord (Galatians 1:8-9).

Meditation: David wrote in Psalm 118 that it was better not to put confidence in men or princes. Did he perhaps mean we should trust the Lord more?

Prayer: O God, teach us to trust in thee with all our hearts.

A Sower Sowed Seed
Mark 4:3-15

"Behold, there went out a sower to sow . . ." (Mark 4:3). In this powerful parable, the sower's seed is the word of God. Found in God's eternal message is the power to grow and produce faith in human hearts. *"Faith comes by hearing, and hearing by the word of God"* (Romans 10:17). Today, it's up to the people of God to sow the seed in the hearts of all so that they may have an opportunity for salvation. Christians are

commanded to take the word of God out into the entire world (Matthew 28:19-20). Jesus lets us know that not everyone will respond favorably to his message (Matthew 7:21-22). Those who do respond begin as babes in Christ. They will need encouragement to walk in the light and fight all the negative influences of this world.

Meditation: Why do you suppose some will never obey the word of God? Why do some remain faithful to the Lord while others do not?

Prayer: Lord, help us to open our eyes to see thy will. O God, teach us to be faithful to thee, even unto death!

Week 19
Lighting Your Candle
Luke 8:16-18

"No man, when he hath lighted a candle, covereth it with a vessel, or putteth it under a bed; but setteth it on a candlestick, that they which enter in may see the light" (Luke 8:16). True Christianity cannot be hidden from others; it will always shine brightly in dark places. When followers of Christ exemplify Christ in their day-to-day lives, then onlookers cannot help but take notice.

A Christ-like life is so noticeable because the attitudes, dispositions, conversations, and reactions that are a part of every Christian's make-up are very different from worldly attitudes and habits. The Christian who hides his or her light from the world will soon discover the flame is flickering and in danger of going out altogether. In the popular children's Bible song, "This Little Light of Mine," important reminders warn us: "Don't let Satan blow it out," and "Don't hide it under a basket."

Meditation: What kind of light was John the Baptizer? Grade the brightness of your Christian light from 1-10, with 10 being the brightest. How bright is your light?

Prayer: Lord, help us to open our eyes to see thy will. O God, teach us to let our lights shine unto others.

Jesus' Family
Luke 8:21

"My mother and my brethren are these which hear the word of God, and do it" (Luke 8:21). Jesus says that when you hear the truth, then do it! At least, that is what a wise man does, according to Matthew 7:24-25. Is it ever enough just to hear the words of God with no further action? Hearing God's message is how faith is acquired (Romans 10:17), and faith always shows itself by good works. It is very important to obey the Lord's commandments (Luke 6:46). Accomplishing God's will today joins us together in a common faith, as one family, the church. The church of Christ, from its infancy until now, is a spiritual family of God, a "New-Israel." Rest assured that God will fulfill his promises to his people just as he did with famous Israel of old (1 Timothy 3:15).

Meditation: Find scriptures that clearly teach what you can do to receive all of the blessings God has promised. How can one be adopted into God's family?

Prayer: Lord, help us to open our eyes to see thy will. O God, teach us to exemplify Christ in our lives!

Where Is Your Faith?
Luke 8:22-25

"Where is your faith?" (Luke 8:25). Sometimes we cannot find our faith when we need it the most. Why is that? Could it be that we have lost our way at least momentarily? Often, we can become so distracted with a tempestuous storm of life that we look away for a moment from the Prince of Peace, the one who can make it all better. Faith demands our attention. It is so important to our salvation that we must never be without it (Hebrews 11:6).

Meditation: What can one do to increase his or her faith? What can one do to keep his or her faith?

Prayer: Lord, teach us to grow in thy grace and knowledge.

What Is Thy Name?
Luke 8:26-36

"What is thy name?" (Luke 8:30). Interestingly, Jesus asks this demonic possessed man his name. Our names say a lot about us. They are the part of us that others recognize when sizing up our character. Every Christian's name is written in God's Book of Life at the moment each one is converted to Christ. Our conversion or obedience in Christ is all about obeying the death, burial, and resurrection of Christ. When this happens we can begin to wear the name Christian, a name given to the early disciples in Acts 11:26. Jesus is, of course, interested in every person, and especially in saving those in Satan's strong hold. He came to seek and save the lost (Luke 19:10) and to free us from our burden of sin.

Meditation: If our own names are important to Christ, then wouldn't the name we use to characterize Christ's church be just as important or maybe more important to him?

Prayer: Lord, teach us to be sure that we follow the path that thou has laid out for us.

God Does Great Things
Luke 8:39-40

"Return to thine own house, and show how great things God hath done unto thee" (Luke 8:39). Here is a clear direction for how every Christian can begin to spread the gospel. Obviously, we can have a greater

influence for good and serve God when Satan's evil influence is no longer a dominating force in our lives. Telling those around us about what God has done for us is the way to do it.

Meditation: Why is it important for us to teach in our own communities and neighborhoods? (Refer to Matthew 28:19.)

Prayer: Lord, let us share the gospel with our neighbors.

Who Touched Me?
Luke 8:43-48

"Somebody hath touched me: for I perceive that virtue is gone out of me" (Luke 8:46). The people were crowding and pressing against Jesus, and his disciples did not understand how he could notice that one woman had touched his clothing and received an instant cure from her long-term disease. Our Lord not only healed her but also acknowledged her faith (vs. 48). Trusting in his power to cure us today can influence the vilest sinner to look to Jesus for the answer to the greatest disease of all— sin.

Meditation: How important is it today to fight against the crowds in an effort to show one's faith? If it is natural for children to want to be close to their fathers just as it is for a loving Father to want to be near his children what can this say about staying in touch with our spiritual Father through Jesus?

Prayer: Lord, lead us to trust in thee for our salvation.

Fear Not: Believe Only?
Luke 8:46-56

"Fear not: believe only, and she shall be made whole [well]" (Luke 8:50). Jesus was on his way to the house of Jairus to heal his sick daughter, but the girl died before Jesus arrived. Imagine the fear and despair Jairus must have felt, and then the relief as Jesus reassured him! Fear can certainly be a determent even to the healthiest faith. Most people struggle with various kinds of fear. One such fear, stage fright, is the fear of speaking in front of others. This fear can immobilize Christians who are frequently on the "stage of life". Whether it is fear, doubt, or something else that hinders our obedience, we can rise to the occasion and show our love for God. In Acts 8:36, a eunuch heard the gospel and asked if anything was hindering him from being baptized (immersed). This good fellow did not allow fear or any other distraction to keep him from his objective: to have his sins washed away. A strong belief helps us to replace a debilitating fear with a healthy one. A fear of God and an assurance in all his promises will help us to accomplish his work with the hope of eternal life.

Meditation: Jesus has ascended into heaven. While we await his second coming, what should we add to belief to receive our salvation? (See Mark 16:16.) What did Solomon say was the whole of man? (See Ecclesiastes 12:13.)

Prayer: Lord, teach us how to demonstrate our faith.

Week 20

Shake off the Dust

Luke 9:1-6

"And whosoever will not receive you, when ye go out of that city, shake off the very dust from your feet for a testimony against them" (Luke 9:6). Disappointment is a part of any worthwhile endeavor. Sadly, some people who decide not to follow Jesus will also have disdain for his followers. But the confident Christian will not allow this to slow him down in his quest to live a faithful Christian life and publish the good news

Meditation: Does this scripture teach us that we should never try again to reach those who have once rejected the truth?

Prayer: Please let us be longsuffering, dear Lord!

The Laborers Are Few

Matthew 9:37-38

"The harvest truly is plenteous, but the laborers are few; Pray ye therefore the Lord of the harvest, that he will send forth laborers into his harvest" (Matthew 9:37-38). More workers for the Lord are always needed. Because his work is so important and far reaching, Christian men and women everywhere are called to participate in his ministry. In Acts 8:6, people went everywhere and shared the good news of human redemption. It is very rewarding to teach another soul the gospel of Jesus Christ and to know

that his or her obedience has created another citizen of heaven. Just one soul is worth more than the entire world. (See Matthew 7:21; Matthew 9:37-38.)

Meditation: Acts 2:39 says "Save yourselves..." How does one do that?

Prayer: Lord, help us to open our eyes to see thy will. O God, we ask humbly for more laborers for thy service!

The Kingdom Is Near
Matthew 10:7

"*. . . The Kingdom of heaven is at hand*" (Matthew 10:7). The true kingdom today without a doubt is the church of Christ. The establishment of the church was imminent at the time of this statement. Later, in Matthew 16:18, we see the first mention of *ecclesia* (church) recorded when Jesus promised to build his church. The fulfillment of this promise would not take place until after the death, burial, resurrection and ascension of Jesus, when the Lord added to the church of Christ the saved for the first time on the Sunday morning of the Day of Pentecost (Acts 2:38-40).

Meditation: Some religious people believe that the kingdom hasn't yet come. Where does scripture tell us otherwise? Which scriptures prove the kingdom and the church to be one and the same?

Prayer: Lord, teach us to respect thine authority above all!

Judgment for a City
Matthew 10:15

"It shall be more tolerable for the land of Sodom and Gomorrah in the day of judgment, than for that city" (Matthew 10:15). Jesus knew his disciples would face resistance when they preached his gospel. The verse given here indicates the severity of the Lord's wrath upon those who know him not on the day of judgment. The people living in the cities and land of Sodom and Gomorrah are described in the Old Testament as being exceedingly wicked. God destroyed these places when ten righteous people could not be found within them. Some sins seem to carry with them a heavier judgment due to greater accountability, but Jesus told his disciples that rejecting the gospel was even worse than the terrible sins of Sodom and Gomorrah. (See Mark 6:10-11; Romans 11:22.)

Meditation: What kinds of sin brought about Sodom and Gomorrah's historically renowned destruction?

Prayer: Please Father, forgive us of every transgression!

Wise as Serpents
Matthew 10:16

". . . be ye therefore wise as serpents and harmless as doves" (Matthew 10:16). Serpents are cunning and crafty while doves are gentle and harmless. In kind, the wise man who reproves should do so gently and

without intent for harm, much like the prophet Nathan when he approached David concerning the king's sin. It was in the form of a dove that the Holy Spirit descended upon Jesus after his baptism. Moreover, Jesus used the innocence of children to portray how Christians today should behave themselves with purity of heart.

Meditation: Why did Jesus use the characterization of a serpent to speak of wisdom? If Jesus said children were innocent of sin, why do some religious groups baptize them? What is the purpose of baptism? What scriptures provided your answer?

Prayer: Lord, teach us to be wise and yet harmless.

The Soul Cannot Die
Matthew 10:28

"And fear not them which kill the body, but are not able to kill the soul: but rather fear him which is able to destroy both soul and body in hell" (Matthew 10:28). To know that a physical life can be cut short and suddenly taken away brings to the mind extreme anxiety and fear. When disease threatens our health or the health of a loved one, there is intense heartache. However, Christians are not to fear these things and can rejoice that their names are written in heaven. In fact, their hardships are described in scripture as moments of "light affliction" (2 Corinthians 4:17). According to Matthew 11:28-30, the "heavy laden" souls that belong to the uninterested or ungodly are deprived of the gifts of purity, spiritual health, comfort, and consolation that

comes from a hope that promises to be an anchor in times of distress and anguish. The Lord teaches that those who deny him can expect to go away and suffer a much deeper sorrow for all of eternity. Christians' have freedom from fear of death because they "rejoice that their names are written in heaven"—a comfort that non-Christians do not have.

Meditation: Please explain the difference between the fear of God and other types of fear.

Prayer: Lord, teach us to have godly fear.

God Knows Everything
Romans 11:33; Ephesians 2:13-20

"But the very hairs of your head are all numbered" (Matthew 10:30). Seven billion people now live on planet earth. God sees everything; he is omnipresent (always everywhere), so there are not any "closet sins" committed by people who may think they have escaped the Lord's notice. Not a single blood pressure can rise one systolic degree or a single hair secretly fall from anyone's head without God knowing. He knows when a sparrow falls to the earth. Adam and Eve were the first people on earth who foolishly attempted to hide themselves from God and failed. The Lord had no problem seeing the prophet Jonah who ran away and tried to hide when he was told to go preach to the great city of Nineveh. It is important to realize that it is impossible to hide from the Lord.

Meditation: Why is it so important to realize that God knows and sees everything?

113

Prayer: Lord, let us face our failures while looking to thee.

Week 21

You are Very Valuable
Matthew 10:31

"Fear ye not therefore, ye are of more value than many sparrows" (Matthew 10:31). God certainly cares for all of his creation, including the animal kingdom. A person may wonder, "Just how many sparrows am I worth?" We love many of God's little creatures, and some are so special to us that we have chosen them as our pets. However, birds along with all the other animals cannot make even one soul-saving choice. Man has been given that gift along with blessings for choosing well and consequences for choosing poorly. Jesus shows us in scripture that even a single soul is worth more to our Father than any person could possibly imagine. (See Matthew 16:24-27; Luke 15.)

Meditation: Why would this knowledge aid us in our resolve not to be afraid?

Prayer: Lord, help us to open our eyes to see thy will. O God, grant us awareness of our vast worth in your eyes!

Confess Him
Matthew 10:32-33

"Whosoever therefore shall confess me before men, him will I confess also before my Father which is in heaven" (Matthew 10:32). Confession is not only good for our souls and consciences, but it also serves another purpose. By confessing our belief courageously before others, we know that Jesus will proudly present us to our Father.

In Acts 8:26-38, the Ethiopian eunuch confessed that he believed Jesus to be the Son of God. Just as in this example, each accountable and believing person must make the same good confession before he or she is permitted to be immersed in baptism for the remission of sins. Both Philip, the evangelist and the eunuch went down into the water so that Philip could baptize the eunuch. After his conversion to Christianity, this new Christian traveled on his way home with great joy in his heart

Meditation: What is mentioned about a person who refuses to confess Jesus before others?

Prayer: Lord, may we never be ashamed of thee!

Peace on Earth
Matthew 10:34

"Think not that I have come to send peace on earth: I came not to send peace, but a sword" (Matthew 10:34). Jesus is the Prince of Peace, but he doesn't force his peace on us. He gives it to us when we choose him as our Savior. Likewise, he doesn't expect us to force his peace or his gospel on anyone. God's word is called the Sword of the Spirit. He uses that sword to achieve his perfect kingdom. Within that kingdom, peace is one of the Christian's most beloved gifts. After receiving it, we are better equipped to become peacemakers. The apostle Paul once alluded to our sense of peace, when he wrote that *"godliness with contentment is great gain"* (1 Timothy 6:6). This can only be achieved when our Peacemaker is our Lord and Savior (Luke 2:14).

Meditation: To whom or to what do many people who are without Christ turn to find peace? When Jesus said he came to send "a sword," instead of peace, what exactly did he mean?

Prayer: Lord, teach us to have inner peace and become peacemakers!

We Have a Cross
Matthew 10:38; Luke 9:23

"And he that taketh not his cross and followeth after me, is not worthy of me" (Matthew 10:38). Jesus carried a crude wooden timber, a cross, to Calvary where soldiers nailed him to it. That cross is now a way of life. It wasn't designed for us to sit on but for us to "take up" and "carry." The Christian life is therefore not an empty-handed religion, but instead, it is an inspired compilation of spiritual concepts that every Christian must learn and practice daily. The Christian works righteousness by letting his light shine, learning along the way to suffer for righteousness as a faithful follower of Jesus Christ. Jesus has invited people to take his yoke and his burden upon themselves and learn of him. Though carrying the cross is hard sometimes, it brings us great hope and joy! It promises us life everlasting and is truly the very best way to live.

Meditation: What does it mean to carry our cross daily? What does the cross represent as we carry it?

Prayer: Lord, give us strength to carry our cross over the finish line!

Finding One's Life
Matthew 10:39-42

"He that findeth his life shall lose it: and he that loseth his life for my sake shall find it" (Matthew 10:40). Jesus explained that selfishness could not rule in his servants. A person who looked for his own "life," instead of searching diligently for Jesus, would lose his life instead of finding it. The straight and narrow path described in Matthew 7:13-14 directs the followers of the Lord to be a people willing to sacrifice many things, even denying self, in order to take hold of eternal life. The sacrifices we make today for the Lord increase our resolve. His providence in our affairs strengthens our trust in him as we hope for a brighter tomorrow.

Meditation: Think of some ideologies that the ungodly of the world have distorted, such as, the fallacy that meekness is the same as weakness.

Prayer: Lord, teach us to give our all to thee!

Preaching to the Poor
Matthew 11:1-6

"The blind receive their sight, and the lame walk, the lepers are cleansed, and the deaf hear, the dead are raised up, and the poor have the gospel preached to them" (Matthew 11:5). Our Lord was active and involved in people's lives. His compassion is undeniable and his love for the down- trodden is

expressed over and over again. He was deeply moved with those who needed to hear the gospel. Today, through the loving message of the gospel, we have available to us the grace of God.

Meditation: Why did Jesus begin with the blind from the list in verse five? Why did he include the poor on the list, but not the rich?

Prayer: Lord, teach us to be more like thy Son, Jesus!

Greater Than John
Matthew 11:7-15

". . . Among them that are born of women there hath not risen a greater than John the Baptist: notwithstanding he that is least in the kingdom of heaven in greater than he" (Matthew 11:11). John the Baptist – who baptized with immersion – was a great prophet, and yet he never became a member of the church of Christ. Sadly, this is because he was executed before the establishment of the church (Acts 2:1-47). John lived and died as a follower of God's Old Covenant Law. The New Testament was taught and defended by the early church of Christ in the first century. Had John lived a few years longer, he could have been numbered with the rank and file, fighting the good fight of faith, along with others that had made it to the Christian Age. However, the blood of Jesus had power to wash away all sins of all the faithful of God, including those who lived before the cross in the Mosaic or Patriarchal ages.

Meditation: Did Jesus indicate in Matthew 11 that he was aware of everyone who was ever born?

Prayer: Lord, teach us to recognize "How Great Thou Art!"

Week 22

Wisdom

Matthew 11:19; Proverbs 3:13-18; 2 Timothy 1:5

". . . *Wisdom is justified of all her children*" (Matthew 11:19). Wisdom is much better than gold or silver. It regenerates and produces offspring. A father and mother can rejoice when, as a result of early training, their child matures into a wise adult. Grandparents can also help to influence their grandchildren positively in the ways of the Lord. The wise man Solomon said, "*Train up a child in the way he should go: and when he is old, he will not depart from it*" (Proverbs 22:6). Hosea reported that in his day, people were destroyed by a lack of knowledge. The young evangelist Timothy was positively influenced by his mother and grandmother who taught him the way of God. We are told in scripture to find wisdom and knowledge. They shout from the pages of God's words.

Meditation: What does the New Testament author James remind us to do if we lack wisdom? What is the difference, if any, in the two terms "wisdom" and "knowledge"?

Prayer: Lord, we ask for wisdom and knowledge!

Repenting Long Ago
Matthew 11:21

"Woe unto thee, Chorazin! Woe unto thee, Bethsaida! for if the mighty works, which were done in you, had been done in Tyre and Sidon, they would have repented long ago in sackcloth and ashes" (Matthew 11:2). When addressing the potential for sin to spread from one place to another, the Apostle Paul wrote, *"a little leaven leaveneth the whole lump"* (1 Corinthians 5:6). Whole cities can be given to idolatry, corruption, or some other desire of the flesh. Since sin is a spiritual disease capable of spreading, it could potentially start in a small place, such as one heart, then one family, one town, and eventually encompass an entire nation. Knowledge of this sin migration can prepare entire congregations to beware of underestimating sin's allurement while diligently exposing its pleasures. Competent Christians know that sin in people's hearts can grow; they remain conscious of this danger and allow themselves instead to *"grow in the grace, and in the knowledge of our Lord and Saviour Jesus Christ"* (2 Peter 3:18). They can examine themselves often to be sure that sin doesn't get a foothold in their own hearts. (See 1 Corinthians 5; Genesis 13.)

Meditation: Jesus said in his most wonderful invitation to "come unto me," because his "yoke was easy and his burden was light." What did he mean when he said his yoke was easy?

Prayer: Lord, teach us to pay less attention to the enticing lures of our enemies!

Come Unto Me
Matthew 11:28-30; 2 Corinthians 4:17; Romans 12:1

"Come unto me, all ye that labor and are heavy laden, and I will give you rest. Take my yoke upon you, and learn of me; . . . and ye shall find rest unto your souls . . . For my yoke is easy, and my burden is light" (Matthew 11:28-30). Many believe that Christianity is just too difficult to attempt and too arduous over the long haul. However, our Lord reveals that, although he does have a yoke and there is a burden to bear, serving God through Jesus Christ is the most reasonable, doable endeavor that exists. The light affliction that all Christians must endure today cannot compare to the eternal glory that awaits them.

Meditation: How successful has Satan been through the years spreading the lie that "the Christian life is too hard to attempt"?

Prayer: Lord, help us to open our eyes to see thy will. O God, teach us to become living sacrifices for thee!

Seeing the Kingdom
Luke 9:27

"But I tell you of a truth, there be some standing here, which shall not taste of death, till they see the kingdom of God" (Luke 9:27). Some standing there on the day Jesus made that statement would also be present on the Day of Pentecost, some fifty days after the Lord's resurrection. They would see – the kingdom as the

church of Christ – for the first time. Saved individuals were being added to the kingdom (the church) by the Lord himself that same day (Acts 2:47). Later, the apostle John would say that he was in the kingdom (church), a clear indication that the church or kingdom was present in his day (Revelation 1:10).

Meditation: Do all who become members of the body of Christ also become citizens of the kingdom?

Prayer: Lord, help us to open our eyes to see thy will. O God, teach us to manage our behavior well within thy kingdom!

Least Shall Be Greatest
Luke 9:48; Luke 9:46-48; Acts 2:38

"Whosoever shall receive this child in my name receiveth me: and whosoever shall receive me receiveth him that sent me: for he that is least among you all, the same shall be great" (Luke 9:48). Every Christian should possess a childlike characteristic of innocence and a pure heart. Since all have *"sinned and fallen short of the glory of God,"* there is an urgent need for every person to repent. Jesus reveals this requirement in Luke 13:3-5, as well as, in other places. For example, the apostle Paul confirms it in Acts 17:30 and thousands were commanded to repent in Acts 2:38.

Meditation: Is humility a childlike quality, or does it only present in those that are mature in their faith?

Prayer: Lord, help us to open our eyes to see thy will. O God, teach us to be more like children in our innocence!

Birds Have Nests
Luke 9:58

"Foxes have holes, and birds of the air have nests; but the Son of man hath not where to lay his head" (Luke 9:58). Birds spend considerable time meticulously constructing their nests. Their purpose is not to sit in them, idling their little lives away, but to care for their young. Jesus gave up the grandeur of heaven to walk the dusty roads of Palestine. He divested himself of the riches of heaven to be financially wanting alongside his disciples. He came to minister to the blind, the crippled, and the hungry instead of asking people to minister to him. (See Luke 9:57-62; Matthew 19:29; Acts 4:34.)

Meditation: Jesus left us an example of giving up riches for a higher purpose. Do you think this is why many do not follow his teachings today? What does Jesus' statement infer about evangelism of the Gospel and the righteousness of the poor today?

Prayer: Lord, help us to open our eyes to see thy will. O God, teach us to make those sacrifices that are pleasing unto thee!

Let Me First Say Goodbye
Luke 9:61

"And another also said, Lord, I will follow thee; but let me first go bid them farewell, which are at home at my house" (Luke 9:61). At first glance, this statement from a would-be follower seems reasonable, but Jesus used it to teach a valuable lesson from a unique perspective. His mission was not just important; it was urgent. What could be more important and more urgent than the salvation of souls? The gospel of Jesus Christ has the power to save men and women everywhere, so it deserves to be preached everywhere. The potential disciple did not understand the urgency of offering salvation to lost souls.

Meditation: Is the Lord saying that some endeavors are more urgent and important than others? Please support your answer with biblical proof.

Prayer: O God, teach us to recognize the urgency of spreading the gospel.

Week 23

Looking Back

Luke 9:62; 2 Peter 2:20-22

"No man having put his hand to the plough, and looking back, is fit for the kingdom of God" (Luke 9:62). Generally, having second thoughts about many things just seems to be a natural part of life. According to Jesus' statement here, however, one should never second guess his or her decision to follow Jesus. The Christian who constantly looks back seldom commits to moving forward. Trusting in our Lord's directions is always the proper path to pursue. Sometimes a farmer looks behind him to see if he has made straight furrows. When he looks forward again, he realizes that by turning around, his course strayed, and his most recent work has become crooked or marred. The phrase "having put his hand to the plough" is a commitment to the job of ploughing. Checking to see if the furrow is straight is not the same as breaking a commitment.

Meditation: Is Jesus saying that the farmer in his example is looking back only momentarily, or has he stopped ploughing?

Prayer: Lord, help us to open our eyes to see thy will. O God, may we never lose our ability to look ahead as we press forward.

The Church Is of Christ
Matthew 12:6; Matthew 12:1-8

"But I say unto you, That in this place is one greater than the temple" (Matthew 12:6). Jesus was greater than the temple. It is not uncommon for importance and emphasis to be placed on some observable aspect of the creation rather than on the Creator. We can often observe the kind of reasoning mentioned here in Matthew 12:6 when encountering those who love nature and yet have no connection with the one who created it all. Similarly, the object of our worship today is not the church building but rather the Creator, Founder, and Builder of the collective members of the church (body) of Christ. The temple was to be the place of worship until the time the church was established on the Day of Pentecost in Acts 2:47. After that first Sunday morning, worshippers came together on the first day of every week to break bread and worship in Spirit and Truth.

Meditation: Do you think the scripture cited above is about giving people permission to worship however they want? Does this attitude permit Christians to consistently commit to being present for daily work and yet excuse themselves from the Lord's day assemblies?

Prayer: Dear Lord God, teach us to understand and practice thy words.

A Divided House
Matthew 12:25-30

"Every kingdom divided against itself is brought to desolation; and every city or house divided against itself shall not stand" (Matthew 12:25). Division is a detriment to unity and robs families of peace. Religious division is condemned in many places in scripture. In John 17 the Lord prayed that his disciples would be united. It is through righteousness that a house, a country, a family, a man, and even a congregation can be exalted; but sin is a reproach to any people. Careful attention should be paid to the peaceful pursuit of unity within the body of Christ. Someone once observed that Noah probably needed to pay closer attention to the beavers and woodpeckers inside the ark than to the raging flood outside. It is true that a closer inspection of one's spiritual health might uncover some needed areas of improvement. James reminds his readers about that when he said *"a double minded man is unstable in all his ways"* (James 1:8; 4:8).

Meditation: How important is this teaching with respect to guiding one's home? What house rules could one adopt that would help prevent division in the home?

Prayer: O God, teach us to have peace within our hearts and homes!

Blasphemy
Matthew 12:24-32

"Wherefore I say unto you, All manner of sin and blasphemy shall be forgiven unto men: but the blasphemy against the Holy Ghost shall not be forgiven unto men. And whosoever speaketh a word against the Son of man, it shall be forgiven him: but whosoever speaketh against the Holy Ghost, it shall not be forgiven him, neither in this world, neither in the world to come" (Matthew 12:31-32). Blasphemy against the Holy Ghost included the accusation brought forward against Jesus that he was using the power of Satan to cast out devils; the Pharisees said he had an unclean spirit, thus denying he was the Son of God. This sin and its consequences were addressed within the Mosaic system of law and pardon (Hebrews 10:1-6). Today, the sin of rejecting the counsel of God results in the same ultimate punishment, separation from God. However, in the New Testament, every sin can receive atonement because of the power found in the blood of Jesus. If we confess our sins, he is faithful and just to forgive us and cleanse us from ALL unrighteousness (1 John 1:7). Notice "all unrighteousness" is a complete rather than partial remedy.

Meditation: Are there any sins today that are impossible for God to forgive? Why is it still impossible to restore some to repentance today?

Prayer: O God, teach us to understand more about thy power!

Good Treasure
Matthew 12:35

"A good man out of the good treasure of the heart bringeth forth good things: and an evil man out of the evil treasure bringeth forth evil things" (Matthew 12:35). Jesus said that we can have good treasure in our hearts. He describes two kinds of trees: a good tree and an evil one. The two trees represent both kinds of people on the earth. Individuals are recognized by their fruits or deeds. These fruits include both words and works, which accounts for the reason Jesus said that all words, good or evil, come from the abundance of one's heart (Matthew 12:33-35; Matthew 5:16; Genesis 2:9, 17; Matthew 6:21).

Meditation: Why did Jesus use the term "treasure" to describe both good and evil words and deeds?

Prayer: Lord, help us to open our eyes to see thy will. O God, teach us to lay up good treasures in heaven!

Every Idle Word
Matthew 12:36-37

"But I say unto you, that every idle word that men shall speak, they shall give account thereof in the day of judgment. For by thy words thou shalt be justified, and by thy words thou shalt be condemned" (Matthew 36-37). Jesus warns that our words can actually save or condemn us at the judgment because they demonstrate either a pure or impure heart. With the

grace of God, we can surely have the fruits of the Spirit. We should purify our hearts, speech, and works through obedience to his word. We must be willing to make all necessary changes. If we can change our thinking in this way; we can simultaneously change our lives and our destinies from hopelessness to hopefulness.

Meditation: What is an example of an idle word? When are we justified with our words?

Prayer: Lord, grant us to see thy will. O God, provide us the wisdom to guard our mouths against foolish speaking!

Greater Than Solomon
Matthew 12:42-45

"The queen of the south shall rise up in the judgment with this generation, and shall condemn it: for she came from the uttermost parts of the earth to hear the wisdom of Solomon; and behold, a greater than Solomon is here" (Matthew 12:42). The queen of the south referenced here was likely Queen of Sheba from Ethiopia, Africa. She had heard about Solomon, as his fame spread worldwide, and so she determined to travel to see for herself if the fascinating reports she had heard were true. We can admire the queen's determination to know the truth about the great king. Sometimes we should put forth more effort to know about someone instead of believing only what we hear about them. Since Jesus' wisdom surpassed all of

Solomon's wisdom, shouldn't people in every nation want to come and learn more about him?

Meditation: When Jesus was only twelve, he fascinated the doctors of the law with his knowledge. If Jesus had more knowledge than King Solomon then why did Jesus wait until he was thirty to begin His ministry?

Prayer: Lord, help us to open our eyes to see thy will. O God, teach us to grow in wisdom by looking more closely at Christ!

Week 24

God's Family
Matthew 12:46-50

"For whosoever shall do the will of my Father which is in heaven, the same is my brother, and sister, and mother" (Matthew 12:50). God's spiritual family is much like our own families. A strong relationship based on love exists throughout the lifetime of the family. In the same way, it is not enough just to think about loving Jesus. Each person must also make a life-long commitment to follow Jesus. Having decided to obey him, every person joins together in one glorious "sheepfold," one spiritual family. We are enjoined to love, trust, and obey by "endeavoring to keep the unity of the Spirit in the bond of peace" (Ephesians 4:3; Matthew 7:21-22; John 10:15-18).

Meditation: Why do some religious people think they know God when God says he doesn't know them? What does the "one body" phrase in Ephesians 4:4 represent?

Prayer: Lord, help us to open our eyes to see thy will. O God, teach us to examine ourselves to be sure we are actually in the faith!

Keeping Secrets
Mark 4:21-23

"For there is nothing hid, which shall not be manifested; neither was anything kept secret, but that it should come abroad" (Mark 4:22). The wise man Solomon said long ago that the eyes of the Lord are everywhere. There are no private matters, sins, or secrets that can remain hidden from the Lord. A crook might be successful in hiding from law enforcement today, but he can never evade the Lord's perfect justice system. The Bible is clear: we can begin to lay up treasures in heaven, but when we refuse to believe and obey our Lord and embrace the darkness here on earth, our deeds will find us out. After their attempt to hide from God among the trees of the garden, Adam and Eve revealed their sin to the only one that could help them. The Lord is merciful, yet just; he will bring every unforgiven sin and evil work into judgement.

Meditation: Why do you suppose secret sins can be so attractive to us? Do you think this could be why pornography is so popular?

Prayer: Lord, help us to open our eyes to see thy will. O God, teach us to confess our faults one to another!

The Mustard Seed
Mark 4:30-32

"And he said, Whereunto shall we liken the kingdom of God? Or with what comparison shall we compare it? It is like a grain of mustard seed, which, when it is sown in the earth, is less than all the seeds that be in the earth; But when it is sown, it growth up, and becometh greater than all herbs, and shooteth out great branches; so that the fowls of the air may lodge under the shadow of it" (Mark 4:30-32). In this parable, the kingdom of God overshadows every other kind of kingdom. Faith is required to be in God's kingdom, (the church), today. This faith is compared to a very small seed that is planted and continues to grow until it is mature enough to help support other life. In nature, the vegetable kingdom gives to the animal kingdom; in turn, the animal kingdom eventually contributes back to nature. One lesson we might learn from this amazing process is that a diligent faith continues to grow. Another lesson is that the type of faith demonstrated within someone's life can continue to be an influence on others for good. What other spiritual conclusions can we draw from this verse?

Meditation: Why does the Lord use one of the smallest seeds for his illustration? Who are the least in the kingdom of God?

Prayer: Lord, help us to open our eyes to see thy will. O God, teach us to have our priorities in proper order!

Peace Be Still
Mark 4:35-41

"And he arose, and rebuked the wind, and said unto the sea, Peace be still. And the wind ceased, and there was a great calm. And he said unto them, Why are ye so fearful? How is it that ye have no faith?" (Mark 4:39-40). Jesus had power to calm the storm, but his disciples needed faith to believe in his power. Noah built an ark before the rain began to fall. In fact, it may have never rained before. It is a good idea to be prepared before the storm approaches. Faith can give us peace and quiet, as it is the ingredient most essential to the art of being calm and still. Our faith, like that of Noah's, must rest on God's promises. The Lord has power over nature and is able to deliver us from any trouble. When the tempest is raging, we can have full assurance in the master of the sea. Furthermore, it is to our advantage to choose to be in his boat.

Meditation: If we had lived in Noah's day, how could we have been saved from the flood? What can we do today to be saved from our sins and from the destruction promised at the end of this world?

Prayer: Lord, teach us to be better prepared for the storms of life!

Friendship Evangelism
Mark 5:19-23

"Go home to thy friends, and tell them how great things the Lord hath done for thee, and hath had compassion on thee" (Mark 5:19). We will have a stronger impact for good upon our friends only when they see in us a better behavior from a significant change of heart. In Biblical times changed hearts were plainly evident when people within their own communities described the great things the Lord had done for them. The Bible is full of examples of people being influenced by the presence of God in other people's life. After they heard and accepted the teachings of Christ, first century disciples began showing improved behavior to those who knew them. Friendship evangelism was successful then and is still influential today!

Meditation: If we want to help save another person, is it ever enough just to be a good example? How does one acquire faith? Use Romans 10:17 for a reference.

Prayer: Lord, help us to open our eyes to see thy will. O God, please give us the desire to help save others!

Prophet without Honor
Mark 6:1-6

"A prophet is not without honor, but in his own country, and among his own kin, and in his own house" (Mark 6:4). Sometimes people have little influence with their own families. Familiarity may hinder our progress in passing along true wisdom to those we know personally. When they heard of Jesus, people in his hometown said, "Is not this the carpenter, the son of Mary, the brother of James?" Though some knew Jesus only as "the carpenter," his followers today know him as the Christ, the Son of the living God. He was the carpenter who carried the wood for our sacrifice; he was nailed to the cross for our remission of sins.

Meditation: What are some things Christians can do to influence those closest to them?

Prayer: Lord, help us to open our eyes to see thy will. O God, teach us to be busy with your works!

Rest a While
Mark 6:30-33

"Come ye yourselves apart into a desert place, and rest a while" (Mark 6:31). Being a workaholic may be preferable for some, but it can often lead to poor health and early retirement. Jesus, who was perfect, showed us that it is always smart to include time for quality rest along the way in order to head out again with a renewed interest and fervor. Quality time may

look quite different depending on everyone's various needs. Time alone, family time, retreats, or nature walks may help to restore some much wanted tranquility. Balance is key to working long term for the Lord. *"There remaineth a rest for the people of God"* (Hebrews 4:9).

Meditation: How did Jesus feel about people coming to him as he retreated to rest awhile?

Prayer: Lord, help us to open our eyes to see thy will. O God, teach us to be wise with the use of our time!

Week 25
Wrong Worship
Mark 7:6-8

"In vain do they worship me, teaching for doctrines the commandments of men" (Mark 7:7). Sadly, those who teach about Jesus today often teach doctrines (teachings that add to, subtract from or substitute for the truth) that are not found in the word of God. As a result, their followers pattern their worship after teachings that do not have the Lord's approval. For example, some religious people teach that baptism is not necessary for one's salvation. However, Jesus himself clearly said in Mark 16:16, "He that believeth and is baptized shall be saved. . . ."

Meditations: Name two other doctrines or teachings that are prevalent today and give evidence from the

Bible that proves them false. What did our Lord say about being able to prove the things that we believe?

Prayer: Lord, help us to open our eyes to see thy will. O God, commit us to teach only thy truth!

Your Traditions
Mark 7:6-16; Galatians 1:1-10

"Making the word of God of none effect through your tradition which ye have delivered: and many such like things do ye" (Mark 7:13). While some traditions are wholesome and even helpful, traditions that circumvent foundational or fundamental truths should never be esteemed superior to biblical doctrine. Tampering with the effectiveness of God's word and his doctrine is a serious business. A clear message from the Holy Scriptures in Revelation 22:18-19 warns us not to add to, subtract from, or pervert the gospel of Jesus Christ.

Meditation: Can you think of any traditions today that interfere with true worship? Do they make the power of God's word ineffective? Do they help us to obey the word of the Lord?

Prayer: Lord, help us to open our eyes to see thy will. O God, teach us to seek God with all of our hearts!

Evil Thoughts
Mark 7:21-23

"For from within, out of the heart of men, proceed evil thoughts, adulteries, fornications, murders, thefts, covetousness, wickedness, deceit, lasciviousness, an evil eye, blasphemy, pride, foolishness; All these evil things come from within, and defile the man" (Mark 7:21-23). Who would deny that having a good heart is priceless? Jesus always promoted the importance of it. His power, demonstrated through his teaching, is designed to create good hearts in all who will give their lives to him. The long list of sins in Mark 7 describes the evil things men dwell on in their hearts, whereby they are defiled. It is vital for every one's spiritual wellbeing to put these sins away in order to improve their standing with God and to allow better thoughts to grow.

Meditation: The Bible teaches that people have an "inner man." To locate a scripture on this topic, use a Bible dictionary or an online search for a key word like "inner" or "inner man."

Prayer: Lord, help us to open our eyes to see thy will. O God, teach us to feed our inner persons with a good diet!

Don't Like What Satan Likes!
Mark 8:31-33

"*Get thee behind me, Satan: for thou savourest not the things that be of God, but the things that be of men*" (Mark 8:33). By keeping Satan behind us and God in front of us, we can follow God more easily and realize our long term goal of reaching heaven. Paul encouraged Christians to move forward with their lives by forgetting the things that were "behind" them, and then, as if in a race for their lives, he told them to "reach ahead." It is easy to be too involved with the "things of yesterday" and too worried about the "things of tomorrow". This focus on temporary things is certainly unnecessary and can hinder a fulfilled Christian life. Seeking those things that are above and "laying up for ourselves treasures in heaven" will have us looking at both our daily and long-term priorities in the proper light.

Meditation: What does "savourest" mean? What word can you think of that we use more often today to describe the same idea?

Prayer: Lord, help us to open our eyes to see thy will. O God, teach us to set our affections on things above!

Consider Your Soul
Mark 8:34-38

"*For what shall it profit a man, if he shall gain the whole world, and lose his own soul? Or what shall a man give in exchange for his soul?*" (Mark 8:36-37). No better question ever prompted man more to consider his own worth. Unfortunately, some substitute earthly things like wealth and worldly pleasures as their most prized possessions. If they lose their own souls, they forfeit their eternal inheritance. When Paul, the beloved apostle, realized that the time of his departure had arrived, he explained that he was ready to die for the Lord was able to keep that which was committed to him. He knew Paradise would soon be his new home; there he would await the Great Judgement and look forward to Heaven, his forever home.

Meditation: What are some things people are giving in exchange for their souls?

Prayer: Lord, help us to open our eyes to see thy will. O God, teach us to protect ourselves from eternal ruin!

Judge Righteously
John 7:21-24

"*Judge not according to the appearance, but judge righteous judgment*" (John 7:24). Some mistakenly believe that Christians aren't allowed to judge anything. But according to Jesus' statement here, we understand that we are indeed commanded to judge, but to do so righteously. We should always remember that it is easy to rush to conclusions or judgements before knowing all the facts, which is a sure sign that we are in danger of judging by appearances only. For these reasons, we should be careful to hear both sides of a story before giving advice or judging someone too critically and before drawing unfounded conclusions about others. On the day of judgment, the word of God will judge everyone (Matthew 7:1-2).

Meditation: Can you give at least one example of a time when we should not judge? When should we judge?

Prayer: Lord, help us to open our eyes to see thy will. O God, let us learn not to judge according to appearances.

Rivers of Living Water
John 7:37-38

"If any man thirst, let him come unto me and drink. He that believeth on me, as the scripture hath said, out of his belly shall flow rivers of living water" (John 7:37-38). When a man decides to forsake everything and follow the Savior, he will be able to do all things through Christ. He will no longer be a little tributary or stream, but rather, a large river which provides for and nourishes many. This is accomplished with the help of the Holy Spirit and made possible only by following God's will for man within the inspired word of God.

Meditation: How can we help ourselves and others create a thirst for the living water that Jesus mentions in this passage?

Prayer: Lord, help us to open our eyes to see thy will. O God, teach us to hunger and thirst after righteousness!

Week 26
Cast the First Stone
John 8:7-11

"He that is without sin among you, let him first cast a stone at her" (John 8:7). There was only one that day who had the right to lift a stone against her, but our Lord chose mercy. Should we not do the same? Jesus admonished her to go and sin no more. Today, some seek and receive mercy from the Lord, but instead of heeding the Lord's warning, they continue in sin. Sinful attitudes and lifestyles are condemned and will always face the force of the Lord's justice. See for yourself by going to Romans 6:1-2.

Meditation: Does having mercy on others mean we should never try to correct any person's wrong doing? Are we ever our brother's keeper?

Prayer: Lord, help us to open our eyes to see thy will. O God, teach us to show mercy unto others!

The Light of the World
John 8:8-12

"I am the light of the world: he that followeth me shall not walk in darkness, but shall have the light of life" (John 8:12). One who wants to see clearly in a world of darkness must follow the lighted way. Christ is the light that can illuminate every person's path. The Bible represents the whole world as a dark and wicked place, though men may not see it that way.

144

Light represents the gospel – the good news – that involves more than what is recorded in the gospels of Matthew, Mark, Luke, and John. All of the truth is necessary if we would be free from sin and grow in the knowledge of God. The truth shows us how to proceed and to succeed when other ways have failed (Matthew 5:16).

Meditation: What did Jesus say would happen when the blind lead the blind? What did He say about people hiding their light?

Prayer: Lord, help us to open our eyes to see thy will. O God, teach us to let our lights shine unto the world!

I Am from Above
John 8:21-26

"Ye are from beneath; I am from above: ye are of this world; I am not of this world. I said therefore unto you that ye shall die in your sins: for if ye believe not that I am he, ye shall die in your sins" (John 8:23-24).

Jesus uses two interesting phrases; which are: "of this world" and "not of this world." They describe the difference between righteousness and unrighteousness, between the spiritual and the worldly. Later we are told that Christians are in the world but never of the world. What does that mean, exactly? It means that Christians try their best not to be molded or changed by the influences of the world, but instead, they seek to be transformed by the teachings of Christ. On the way to becoming a Christian, individuals must first believe that Jesus is their Savior, they learn that to trust and obey him is as important as it is to hear and believe him.

Meditation: How can a Christian be "in the world" while at the same time "not of the world"? Please give an example. What does a person fitting this description look like today?

Prayer: Lord, help us to open our eyes to see thy will. O God, help us not to be followers of the world!

Truth Makes You Free
John 8:31-32

"If ye continue in my word, then are ye my disciples indeed; And ye shall know the truth, and the truth shall make you free" (John 8:31-32). There is nothing like being free from the burden of sin, but it certainly comes with a price. It is expensive; there are conditions and a cost for making the choice! A person who wants freedom from sin's slavery must be a diligent follower of Jesus Christ, must know the truth, be obedient to it, and must continue in God's word; and God's word is always described as being truth itself (John 17:17).

Meditation: How are knowing the truth and continuing in the word of God related? Are there other ways the truth can make us free?

Prayer: Lord, help us to open our eyes to see thy will. O God, admonish us to know the truth that makes us free!

Older Than Abraham?
John 8:58

"Verily, Verily, I say unto you, before Abraham was, I am" (John 8:58). Jesus revealed his earlier existence and eternal nature when he said that he was older than Abraham. We know from the Bible that Jesus was with God his Father before the creation of the earth and that "all authority" was given to him. The implication is that the Jews should be looking to him for spiritual guidance instead of Abraham or Moses. Jesus also showed his durability and power when he referenced the prophet Jonah to inform his audience that one "greater than Jonah" was present.

Meditation: How did Jesus' answer affect those who heard it? Is there a lesson in that for us today?

Prayer: Lord, help us to open our eyes to see thy will. O God, teach us to be constantly looking to thee!

Dull of Hearing
Matthew 13:11-17

"For this people's heart is waxed gross, and their ears are dull of hearing, and their eyes they have closed; lest at any time they should see with their eyes and hear with their ears, and should understand with their heart, and should be converted and I should heal them" (Matthew 13:15). Carelessness is kin to callousness. It is possible for an entire group, even a nation of people, to become so calloused in their hearts that they willingly close their eyes and ears to the truth.

147

The good news is that there is an all-healing cure. Even today, the Great Physician has the remedy for the worst disease of them all: sin! Knowing that each of our souls is worth more than the whole world, why would we linger or close our hearts?

Meditation: What does a person have to do to find faith today? (Refer to Romans 10:17.)

Prayer: Dear Lord, teach us to have the kind of faith that will save us.

Kingdom Is like Leaven
Matthew 13:33; 1 Corinthians 5:1-10

"The kingdom of heaven is like unto leaven which a woman took, and hid in three measures of meal, till the whole was leavened" (Matthew 13:33). The kingdom of God, which is the church today, must reach out and go forth spreading seed of the gospel throughout the whole world, influencing others, and causing men to rise up to righteousness. This reaching out is demonstrated through the lips and hearts of every faithful child of God.

Meditation: Please find in your Bible where it is said that "the whole world lieth in wickedness" (darkness). What is the logical thing to say to those searching the whole world for something better?

Prayer: O God, teach us how to put on our Lord and Savior.

Week 27
A Hidden Treasure
Matthew 13:37-58

"Again, the kingdom of heaven is like unto treasure hid in a field; the which when a man hath found, he hideth, and for joy thereof goeth and selleth all that he hath, and buyeth that field" (Matthew 13:44). Jesus paid it all; therefore, Christians are expected to give their all! The man in this parable is so excited with what he has found that he sells all that he has in order to gain the treasure. Just so, Christians are excited about their Christianity and give all to gain the great treasures it brings. They are willing to cast off to new territory or "launch out unto the deep" to put down their nets and put off their "old things" to obtain their crown of life (2 Corinthians 5:17). Christianity is sacrificial; it will cost us everything. We will give our all, but it will be more than worth it, as we live a promised abundant life now and gain our inheritance later.

Meditation: Why is Christianity so expensive? Why do some who profess Christianity seem bored and out of touch?

Prayer: Lord, help us to open our eyes to see thy will. O God, teach us to have the zeal of thy Son Jesus, along with the knowledge to apply it to benefit thee!

Having Honor at Home
Matthew 13:53-58

"A prophet is not without honor, save in his own country, and in his own house" (Matthew 13:57). Jesus gives advice to those who attempt to teach their friends and family. No matter how powerful the message or how famous the messenger, listeners are often unimpressed. Many were offended at Jesus for simply speaking the truth. Sometimes, strangers have the evangelical advantage among our closest associates.

Meditation: Can Christians ever feel they have no honor or respect? What can they do at such times?

Prayer: O Lord, teach us to never ever give up!

Small Faith
Matthew 14:31

"O thou of little faith, wherefore didst thou doubt?" (Matthew 14:31). "Doubt" and "little faith" seem to be the best of friends! James writes that if we pray for something, we shouldn't doubt that God can answer that prayer (1:6). Doubt is difficult to push aside or erase, though one might try by addressing doubt with positive reinforcement, such as simply remembering a time in the past when prayer was the perfect answer to an otherwise impossible problem. When he was about to fight the giant Goliath, David remembered how the Lord had helped him defeat both a lion and bear in the past. Knowing God was

with him must have helped him run to meet the giant and defeat him for the armies of the Israelites and for God's glory.

Meditation: How might one go about building more faith and diminishing doubt?

Prayer: O God, teach us to enjoy all of our spiritual blessings!

Weeds Are Plants, Too
Matthew 15:13

"Every plant, which my heavenly Father hath not planted, shall be rooted up" (Matthew 15:13). Here the Lord has in mind his kingdom. Using a very familiar farming analogy, he portrays a much deeper meaning. He implies that individuals have gone about planting things that are offensive to him. But how exactly is this done? By planting counterfeit seeds or plants, it might be possible to deceive some inexperienced gardeners but not an experienced farmer (Galatians 1:1-10). Remember that the true seed is the word of God, and that pure truth produces good trees or plants that bear good or righteous fruit. Even though some plants may look like the real thing, they prove to be counterfeits. It was just as important in the first century, as it still is today, that people are able to discern between the plants God has planted and the ones he has not.

Meditation: What does the phrase "every plant" represent today? When is rooting season?

Prayer: O God, help us recognize every true plant.

Blind Leaders
Matthew 15:14

"Let them alone: they be blind leaders of the blind. And if the blind lead the blind, both shall fall into the ditch" (Matthew 15:14). Religious people will follow religious leaders! However, it is necessary to pay attention to where those leaders have been and where they are going. Some teach a gospel of wealth, another of health, of faith healing, of tongue speaking, or of snake handling, etc. Religion will hinder one's spirituality when it obscures the concept of "real" truth. Just going through the motions is robotic, not real or heartfelt!

Meditation: How can a person feel closer to God? Is feeling closer to God the same as being close to him?

Prayer: Lord, O God, help us to recognize and turn from blind leaders.

The Sky Is Red
Matthew 16:2-3

"When it is evening, ye say, It will be fair weather: for the sky is red. And in the morning, It will be foul weather today: for the sky is red and lowering. O ye hypocrites, ye can discern the face of the sky; but can ye not discern the signs of the times?" (Matthew 16:2-

3). Being able to observe nature and notice the environmental changes is truly helpful and to observe shifts in beliefs and culture has merit. Even so, to be aware of one's own spiritual condition is of far greater value. The Prophet Jonah heralded throughout Nineveh that its citizens should all repent! Sometimes ignorance will keep us from fulfilling all of God's will for us; but to know the truth will set us free!

Meditation: Why are some spiritual things more difficult to see than physical things?

Prayer: Lord, O God, teach us thy truth.

I Will Build My Church
Matthew 16:18

"And I say also unto thee, That thou art Peter, and upon this rock I will build my church; and the gates of hell shall not prevail against it" (Matthew 16:18). Our Lord Jesus is here promising to build his church. Notice the singularity of the one church he would establish when he refers to it as "my church." This is the first time the Bible refers to *ecclesia,* the Greek word meaning "assembly" or church. Romans 16:16 also refers to Christ's church, but this time in the plural as the "churches of Christ," to reference many congregations of the same kind of church.

Meditation: Why is the idea of the singularity of Christ's church so important?

Prayer: Lord, help us to know more about thy church.

Week 28

Jesus Pays Tax
Matthew 17:24-27

"Notwithstanding, lest we should offend them, go thou to the sea, and cast an hook, and take up the fish that first cometh up; and when thou hast opened his mouth, thou shalt find a piece of money; take that, and give unto them for me and thee" (Matthew17:27). Jesus reveals that tax collection in the first century was unfair and full of prejudice; however, he also shows us that it is important to obey the laws of the land. He further drives home this point on a separate occasion, when he says to give unto Caesar the things that belong to Caesar. Notice, he doesn't take money from any of the donations that they may have received from their ministry, possibly showing a "restricted use" status of this income.

Meditation: How would you answer someone who feels justified not paying taxes, stating that the government uses his tax contributions to promote ungodly agendas?

Prayer: Lord, O God, teach us to obey the laws of the land and thereby be good citizens!

Names in Heaven
Luke 10:17-20

"Notwithstanding in this rejoice not, that the spirits are subject unto you; but rather rejoice, because your names are written in heaven" (Luke 10:20). Often a Christian can lose sight of the bigger picture. The disciples had enjoyed success and saw Christianity winning; good had triumphed over evil. Jesus praised the good work they had done, but said they should rejoice more because of their eternal inheritance. The Lord had given them power over evil spirits, but he wanted them to focus more on the long term goal. The evil spirits the disciples had conquered had no hope for the future, but the righteous would live with God in an eternal paradise.

Meditations: What happens when one resists the devil and his minions today?

Prayer: Lord, O God, teach us to finally open our "eyes of faith" much wider than ever before!

Who Is My Neighbor?
Luke 10:30-37

"Which now of these three, thinkest thou, was neighbor unto him that fell among thieves?" (Luke 10:36). Jesus teaches that our neighbor could be anyone. Since there is an unexpected consequence associated with misfortune, and since bad things can happen by chance, God's children should always be prepared to

give aid to anyone at any time. Life's uncertainty can have us on the receiving end of those bad things. Every Christian has assurance about the unknown and is prepared for tomorrow and should not be afraid or worried about the future. (See Matthew 6:34.)

Meditation: Since our neighbors are everyone and everywhere, who then is our enemy?

Prayer: Merciful Father, teach us to love our neighbors and our enemies!

Martha, Martha
Luke 10:38-42

"Martha, Martha, thou art careful and troubled about many things: But one thing is needful: and Mary hath chosen that good part, which shall not be taken away from her" (Luke 10:41-42). Jesus calls Martha's name twice. Maybe it was to help her to turn her attention to him. Choosing to focus on the best parts of life will often help us to avoid the worst parts of life. Martha was busy, and she wanted Jesus to tell her sister to help her. It is easy to focus only on the things we feel are important in the moment, but the Lord reminds Martha of the thing that was the most important. By being more in tune with spiritual things, we will be less concerned about all the things we sometimes falsely find so attractive.

Meditation: What are some ways that Christians today can choose to focus on the "good part"?

Prayer: Dear God, teach us to choose to focus more on the good part!

Gifts to Our Children
Luke 11:9-13

"If ye then, being evil, know how to give good gifts unto your children: how much more shall your heavenly Father give the Holy Spirit to them that ask him" (Luke 11:13). As a parent, we usually want to give good things to our children even when they don't ask for them. Here we see the Holy Spirit is given to those who ask. No doubt this is in reference to one of the twelve miraculous gifts given later to some of Christ's servants. It could also refer to the Holy Spirit being the gift given to all who obey the Lord's plan of salvation as explained in Acts 2:38-39. The good Lord certainly knows how to give good gifts to all of his children.

Meditation: Who from the Old Testament received two things that he hadn't prayed for? What did he receive?

Prayer: Lord, help us to open our eyes to see thy will. O God, may we seek thee with our whole heart!

Keeping His Palace
Luke 11:14-26

"When a strong man armed keepeth his palace, his goods are in peace" (Luke 11:21). This divine instruction from Christ later had great influence on the Apostle Paul's ministry. It reminds Christians that strength is from the Lord, and they must keep their faith if they hope to enjoy a bountiful inheritance. The inspired writing of Paul encourages us today that Christians can use this strength to do all things through Christ (Philippians 4:13).

Meditation: What kinds of things did Jesus do to show his perfect strength?

Prayer: Lord, help us to fill our palaces with good things.

Giving
Luke 11:41-42

"But rather give alms of such things as ye have; and, behold, all things are clean unto you" (Luke 11:41). Giving from what we have been given is one of the most basic of all Christian privileges. Not only is giving required of every faithful child of God, but it should also be done freely and cheerfully from the heart. Some religiously sincere individuals boast of giving tithes of their income while completely neglecting many other important commands, such as the command of baptism for remission of sins (John 14:15). It is extremely important to obey every New Testament commandment.

Meditation: Do you suppose giving is any more important than the other activities we do in our Sunday worship? Why do you think some uphold it as a priority, and yet fail to include other important things like the observance of the Lord's Supper as seen in Acts 20:7?

Prayer: Lord, O God, may we give purposefully and cheerfully!

Week 29
Invisible Graves
Luke 11:44

"Woe unto you, scribes and Pharisees, hypocrites! for ye are as graves which appear not, and the men that walk over them are not aware of them" (Luke 11:44). The Lord describes these hypocrites as invisible graves. It is a very sad description of those who may have once had very purposeful and righteous lives. Even though they were yet alive, they were dead spiritually. The only greater disappointment was the fact that their sad condition was so well hidden from others!

Meditation: Can we through the spiritual eye glasses of faith see better the invisible things of God? How might that work?

Prayer: Lord, help us to see more invisible things.

Lawyers
Luke 11:46; 2 Timothy 4:6-8

"Woe unto you also, ye lawyers! for ye lade men with burdens grievous to be borne, and ye yourselves touch not the burdens with one of your fingers" (Luke 11:46). Jesus says here that the lawyers of his day were lazy. Christians should never be slothful in their duties. The Hebrew writer mentions being a diligent disciple in Hebrews 11:6. What does a diligent disciple look like today? And how can we be sure that we are true disciples?

Meditation: What Old Testament problem was only solved by delegating the work because it was too great a job for any one person?

Prayer: Dear Lord, may we continue to maintain good works daily!

Fear Him
Luke 12:4-5

"And I say unto you my friends, Be not afraid of them that kill the body, and after that have no more that they can do. But I will forewarn you whom ye shall fear: Fear him, which after he hath killed hath power to cast into hell; yea, I say unto you: Fear him" (Luke 12:4-5). Jesus teaches us whom to fear. He said men can harm the body but are powerless to destroy the soul. Having a healthy fear for the Lord brings our admiration and respect into view. King Solomon once said that men should fear the Lord and keep his

commandments because that was the "whole of man" (Ecclesiastes 12:13-14).

Meditation: The Bible speaks of two types of fear. What are they?

Prayer: Lord, help us not to be so afraid and worried.

Confessing Him
Luke 12:8-9

"Also I say unto you, Whosever shall confess me before men, him shall the Son of man also confess before the angels of God: But he that denieth me before men shall be denied before the angels of God" (Luke 12:8-9). A contrite heart brings us closer to salvation because a heart like that can more easily confess that Jesus is the Son of God. Many came to John the Baptizer to confess their sins. Those seeking salvation today will come confessing him and telling others what the eunuch declared many years ago, that "Jesus Christ is the Son of God" (Acts 8:36). We may never deny him with our lips, but we do so easily by our actions or lack thereof. For instance, some religions teach that by confessing that Jesus is Lord, along with admitting their past transgressions, a person will effortlessly be awarded salvation. However, Jesus himself taught that baptism washes away sin. Therefore, baptism is also necessary to one's salvation and should be an intricate part of a believer's faith.

Meditation: If the Lord requires five activities before he sends his blessing, then are only two or three enough? Would Noah have been obeying God if he chose to use a different building material than the one God specified for him?

Prayer: Lord, help us to do all thy will! Teach us not to fall short of thy satisfaction!

Covetousness
Luke 12:15

"Take heed, and beware of covetousness: for a man's life consisteth not in the abundance of the things which he possesseth" (Luke 12:15). Our possessions can often get in the way of our walk with God. If we are not careful, our possessions can become burdens to us, weighing us down when we are striving to stay the course. The straight gate and the narrow way are accessible, but we must leave the paths of sin and focus on remaining on the path of righteousness. There is a sin that "doth so easily beset us" (Hebrews 12:1). Let us lay these sins aside at the foot of the cross, especially the sin of covetousness.

Meditation: If a man's life doesn't consist of physical things, what does it consist of?

Prayer: Lord, help us to run the race with patience. Teach us not to allow riches to blind us to thee!

Bigger Barns
Luke 12:16-21

"And I will say to my soul, Soul, thou hast much good laid up for many years; take thine ease, eat, drink, and be merry" (Luke 12:19). The parable of the rich farmer offers us many lessons. The conclusion is that whether we are rich or poor, we can always choose to be rich in faith. Putting God first will always help us to seek the true riches of life.

Meditation: Is it always a sin to build a bigger barn? How does the Christian best accomplish the task of having the right focus on money?

Prayer: Lord, help us to seek the true riches of life. Teach us to love thee more as we grow!

Always Be Ready!
Luke 12:35-40

"And this know, that if the good man of the house had known what hour the thief would come, he would have watched, and not have suffered his house to be broken through. Be ye therefore ready also: for the Son of man cometh at an hour when ye think not" (Luke 12:39-40). The Lord Jesus will return one day, though no one knows the exact time (Matthew 12:36). We, as his faithful children, must always be ready! When we are expecting company, we prepare for their arrival. Jesus promised to return, so we must be ready spiritually at all times.

Meditation: When Jesus said the man would not *"suffer his house to be broken through,"* was he saying that we are to have strong houses? Consult Matthew 7:24-29 for your answer.

Prayer: Lord, help us to always be ready to meet thee! Help us to strengthen our foundations and prepare our hearts.

Week 30

Few Stripes or Many
Luke 12:41-48

"And that servant, which knew his lord's will, and prepared not himself, neither did according to his will, shall be beaten with many stripes. But he that knew not, and did commit things worthy of stripes, shall be beaten with few stripes. For unto whomsoever much is given, of him shall be much required: and to whom men have committed much, of him they will ask the more" (Luke 12:47-48). Our Lord pronounces a more stern judgment on those who know of his will and yet still rejects it. This judgement is represented by the number of stripes each offender receives. It is foolish for individuals to choose to remain ignorant of their Lord's will for their lives while they readily have the time and opportunity to learn it.

Meditation: It was through ignorance and envy that Jesus was delivered up to be crucified. How can we avoid envy and ignorance today?

Prayer: Lord, help us to know thy truth so that we can be free! Teach us to share that powerful truth with others!

Accomplishments!
Luke 12:50

"But I have a baptism to be baptized with; and how am I straitened till it be accomplished!" (Luke 12:50). The Lord had already been baptized in the river Jordon, but here he speaks of another baptism. This baptism would be representative of his death on the cross. One might ask, "But what about the thief on the cross?" Does his apparent salvation prove that baptism may not be necessary today for all people for their salvation? Certainly not! The thief's death on the cross was a type of baptism for him. We are crucified with Christ in our baptism (Romans 6:4). Furthermore, the thief was saved before Jesus' death and before New Testament baptism was ever commanded as seen in Acts 2:38, a mere 50 days later on the Day of Pentecost.

Meditation: Since Christ granted salvation for the thief on the cross before he commanded all to be baptized for remission of sins, can anyone today be saved without baptism?

Prayer: Dear God, show us how baptism saves us today!

Getting Sued!
Luke 12:54-59

"When thou goest with thine adversary to the magistrate, as thou art in the way, give diligence that thou mayest be delivered from him; lest he hale thee to the judge, and the judge deliver thee to the officer, and the officer cast thee into prison. I tell thee, thou shalt not depart hence, till thou hath paid the very last mite" (Luke 12:58-59). It is often advisable to settle our differences with someone outside of court. Sometimes it is to our advantage to allow our enemies the final word to this end. In the bigger picture, we know the Judge of mankind is looking on and each of us will appear to give testimony on that great day of judgment (Hebrews 9:27).

Meditation: How would you answer the question Jesus asks in Luke 12:57?

Prayer: Dear Lord, teach us to be wise when we work with others.

Repent
Luke 13:1-5

"Nay: but, except ye repent, ye shall all likewise perish" (Luke 13:3). Repentance is an absolutely essential ingredient for salvation. It is a principle found in both the Old and New Covenants. Supposedly, some thought that these Galileans – along with eighteen others who died infamously – were worse sinners than all others. But Jesus clarifies and reminds them

and us that all will be judged as sinners if they refuse to repent and turn to him in obedience.

Meditation: Some profess that one can turn to the Lord through a simple confession of faith and immediately be in a saved condition. How can this kind of thinking inadvertently misrepresent our Lord to others?

Prayer: Lord, O God, teach us to have penitent hearts in order to turn permanently from our sins!

Cut It Down
Luke 13:6-9

"Then said he to the dresser of his vineyard, Behold, these three years I come seeking fruit on this fig tree, and find none: cut it down; why cumbereth it the ground?" (Luke 13:7). Christians must bear good fruit in order to please the Lord. Thankfully, the Lord is patient and gives his children time and opportunity to produce these good fruits. If a fig tree is expected to bear fruit each season, what does that say about a person who hasn't produced spiritual fruit in three years or longer?

Meditation: What are some reasons and excuses the fig tree could have given, if it had been able to speak, for not bearing fruit? What does "cumbereth" or "cumbered" mean?

Prayer: Lord, O God, may we learn not to make excuses for our disobedience!

Abraham Is Still Alive?
Luke 13:24-30

"There shall be weeping and gnashing of teeth, when ye shall see Abraham and Isaac, and Jacob, and all the prophets, in the kingdom of God, and you yourselves thrust out" (Luke 13:28). While the rich man was in torment in Luke 15:1-32, he saw Abraham in paradise. It appears from this text that Father Abraham speaks on behalf of Lazarus and that we will recognize each other after death. Also apparent from the text is that some will be saved, while others will be lost.

Meditation: On the day of judgment when God separates the righteous from the wicked, what books will be opened?

Prayer: Lord, may we obey thee from true hearts!

I Do Cures
Luke 13:32

"Go ye and tell that fox, Behold, I cast out devils, and I do cures today and tomorrow, and the third day I shall be perfected" (Luke 13:32). Jesus speaks of his resurrection that would occur early on Sunday morning. Later in Acts 20:7, we find the disciples meeting together on a Sunday, the first day of the week, to observe the Lord's Supper in remembrance of this great event. Early disciples were meeting each

first day of the week to worship. (See 1 Corinthians 16:1-2.)

Meditation: Why did Jesus call Herod a fox? Jesus uses this animal in another instance. What was that instance?

Prayer: Lord, O God, teach us to become perfect like thee!

Week 31
O Jerusalem, Jerusalem
Luke 13:34-35; Proverbs 1:20-33

"O Jerusalem, Jerusalem, which killest the prophets, and stonest them that are sent unto thee; how often would I have gathered thy children together as a hen doth gather her brood under her wings, and ye would not" (Luke 13:34). We read in the New Testament that Jesus wept on two occasions: once when his friend Lazarus died, and here as he surveyed the eroded condition of his people. He came to seek and save the lost, but not everyone will accept his gracious gift. We are most safe while under the wing of God through his Son and our Savior, Jesus.

Meditation: Where can one turn if he or she rejects God? Why are some people rebellious and others not?

Prayer: Lord, O God, teach us how to seek thee with our whole hearts!

Sit in the Lowest Room
Luke 14:7-11

"When thou art bidden of any man to a wedding, sit not down in the highest room; lest a more honorable man than thou be bidden of him; And he that bade thee and him come and say to thee, Give this man place; and thou begin with shame to take the lowest room" (Luke 14:8-10). This parable shows that the man who humbles himself will experience less shame in his lifetime than a prideful person. It teaches believers to make proper choices to demonstrate a Christ-like attitude in the presence of others. When men seek only to advance themselves, they no longer resemble our Lord.

Meditation: What promise do we have from the Lord when we humble ourselves?

Prayer: Lord, O God, teach us to be humble of heart.

Dinner for the Poor
Luke 14:12

"When thou makest a dinner or a supper, call not thy friends, nor thy brethren, neither thy kinsmen, and thy rich neighbors; lest they also bid thee again, and a recompense be made. But when thou makest a feast, call the poor, the maimed, the lame, the blind" (Luke 14:12-13). This parable reminds us that our neighbors are everyone, even those who are often neglected. When we begin choosing who to help and who to teach the Gospel, then some go unfed and

uncared for. Jesus said in his Sermon on the Mount that when we love only those who love us, then how are we unlike everyone else? He expects us to love and care for those who will not or cannot return the favor.

Meditation: Give at least two scenarios in which a Christian might put this principle into practice today.

Prayer: Lord, O God, teach us to view everyone, rich and poor, as neighbors!

My House
Luke 14:15-24

"And the Lord said unto the servant, Go out into the highways and hedges, and compel them to come in, that my house may be filled" (Luke 14:23). This parable of the great supper contains many lessons. One such lesson is that the Lord wills that his house, the church, should be inviting to foreign guests and alien sinners who might soon become members of the Lord's family.

Meditation: How important is it not to be prejudiced against those in less desirable situations?

Prayer: Lord, help us not to be prejudiced.

Finish What We Begin
Luke 14:25-32

"For which of you, intending to build a tower, sitteth not down first, and counteth the cost whether he have sufficient to finish it? Lest haply, after he hath laid the foundation, and is not able to finish it, all that behold it begin to mock him, Saying, This man began to build, and was not able to finish" (Luke 14:28-29). Counting the cost is a smart move before attempting any worthwhile project. How much does it cost when it comes to giving one's life to the service of the cross of Christ? Jesus gave us his everything and yet we are sometimes reluctant to give up our everything. It is a commitment to carry our cross for him and please our Father in heaven.

Meditation: What is the reaction today when people see someone who is unable to finish a building project? Could it not also be the same when one decides to no longer follow Jesus?

Prayer: Lord, help us to finish what we begin.

Being a Disciple
Luke 14:33

"So likewise, whosoever he be of you that forsaketh not all that he hath, he cannot be my disciple" (Luke 14:33). Being one of the Lord's disciples requires great commitment. Individuals that share in this level of service must separate themselves from the world

and put him first before all things. Any true disciple of the Lord doesn't pretend to follow him! He must have real faith and be determined to walk in the right direction.

Meditation: Do you believe there are those who are pretending to be children of the Most High? If so, what might motivate them to do such a thing?

Prayer: Lord, God, teach us to commit unto Thee.

Salty
Luke 14:34-35

"Salt is good: but if the salt have lost his savour, wherewith shall it be seasoned? It is neither fit for the land nor yet for the dunghill; but men cast it out. He that hath ears to hear, let him hear" (Luke 14:34-35). Just as salt can lose its saltiness, the Christian can fall from his own steadfastness! When he falls out of "flavor," he falls out of favor with God, and thereby loses his influence with others. Notice Jesus uses the pronoun "his" to show that the salt's seasoning power, "savour" (flavor), belongs to the Christian.

Meditation: Give some examples of when saltiness might be used by a Christian for a higher purpose. Does salt have any healing properties? Describe a Christian with salty "savour."

Prayer: O God, teach us to be Christians with "saltiness."

Week 32
Works of God
John 9:1-34

"Neither hath this man sinned, nor his parents: but that the works of God should be made manifest in him" (John 9:3). It is easy for Christians to think that all of our hard times, problems, and health concerns are a direct result of some kind of sin we have committed. While this could be true occasionally, often these trials are not punishments, but merely opportunities for others to see our resolve. Letting our Christianity shine shows others what the Lord is doing for us. Furthermore, Jesus told us that it rains on the just and on the unjust. Trouble can come to anyone, and we will all have trials in this life. All that live godly lives will suffer some persecution!

Meditation: Why did some think sin caused this man to be born blind? Why did the parents want the officers to ask their son questions?

Prayer: Dear God, teach us to behold all thy wondrous works.

The Lord Is Talking Now
John 9:35-41

"Dost thou believe on the Son of God?" (John 9:35). Being an obedient believer puts us in step with the Savior and out of step with the world or the "in-

crowd." It is a blessing to be unassociated with some groups anyway. However, if we are with the in-crowd, and it happens to be the "in Christ" crowd, then all is well.

Meditation: Give an example of a situation when a person today could be afraid of professing something positive about God or his power.

Prayer: Lord, O God, teach us to be strong in thee, Lord!

Walk This Way
John 10:1-7

"Verily, verily, I say unto you, He that entereth not by the door into the sheepfold, but climbeth up some other way, the same is a thief and a robber" (John 10:1). It is a mistake to think that just any plan of action will please the Lord, even if it comes from the sincerest of hearts, and its end goal is to reach heaven. Because Jesus said he was "the way," there is a very specific outline and plan to follow with a very particular set of directions. There is definitely a pattern found in the scriptures that is God's divine doctrine, and everyone is commanded to follow his important instructions

Meditation: What are the five steps to salvation outlined in the New Testament?

Prayer: Lord, help me to see a spiritual path for me.

I'm the Door
John 10:8-10

"I am the door: by me if any man enter in, he shall be saved, and shall go in and out, and find pasture. The thief cometh not, but for to steal, and to kill, and to destroy: I am come that they might have life, and that they might have it more abundantly" (John 10: 9-10). Noah's ark had only one window and one door; and similarly, the Lord's church (the church of Christ mentioned in Romans 16:16) has one door. Jesus said he came to give life, not take it. Our benevolent God always protects and provides for those who follow him according to his grace and instructions. This is why Noah and his good family were saved from the flood in the primordial world, and it is the same reason we are saved today in our modern world.

Meditation: In the scripture above, who does the thief represent?

Prayer: Lord, O God, may we recognize the thief and protect ourselves with your grace.

The Good Shepherd
John 10:11-15

"I am the good shepherd: the good shepherd giveth his life for the sheep" (John 10:11). A good shepherd is willing, if circumstances demand it, to give his own life for his sheep. Jesus is described as the good Shepherd and did exactly that. He is our Redeemer and head of his church and Bishop of our souls (the

same church of Christ mentioned in Romans 16:16).
He purchased the church and oversees her progress.
We are his one body and his one flock here on the
Earth.

Meditation: How does Jesus communicate with all of
his church leaders today? How do they know what is
best as they minister and provide leadership?

Prayer: Lord, O God, may we seek thee with our
whole hearts!

One Fold

John 10:16; Acts 2:47; Ephesians 5:24-30

*"And other sheep I have, which are not of this fold:
them also I must bring, and they shall hear my voice;
and there shall be one fold, and one shepherd"* (John
10:16). God the Father, Jesus the Son, and the Holy
Spirit have always wanted one sheepfold (Ephesians
4:4). Please notice what Jesus prayed before his
crucifixion in John 17:21. Since Jesus said he had one
flock, why are religious people divided into so many
branches of faith?

Meditation: Is his sheepfold recognizable today?
What are the true sheepfold's identifiable traits?

Prayer: Lord, O God, may we be able to recognize
your sheepfold?

My Sheep

John 10:17-29

"My sheep hear my voice, and I know them, and they follow me" (John 10:27). The voice of the Savior says come (Matthew 11:28). We cannot hear the sound of his voice today, but we can surely hear his message. Unfortunately, he said many will choose not to listen to him! But faith comes by first hearing what Jesus taught (Romans 10:17). Hearing the Lord's saving message is the first step towards one's salvation.

Meditation: How does one grow in faith today? Refer to Romans 10:17 for an accurate answer.

Prayer: Lord, O God, let us open our ears to hear the Savior's call.

Week 33

Unity

John 10:30; Ephesians 4:1-10; John 17

"I and my Father are one" (John 10:30). One of the Biblical names used to describe Jesus is "Immanuel," which means "God with us." Jesus and his Father are united as one through love and purpose. Many close family relationships share a similar bond. When individuals become New Testament Christians today, they are added to the church where they can enjoy a close relationship with God and with one another. The family of God, the church, must always *"endeavor*

to keep unity in the bond of peace." Before Jesus was crucified, he was almost stoned by the unbelieving Jews. Christians who take on the mantle of Christ will undoubtedly also be persecuted for their good works, faith, and service!

Meditation: Why did Paul mention the term "one body" in Ephesians? What does it reference, and how does it relate to unity?

Prayer: O God teach us how best to achieve unity, as we endeavor now to keep it!

Glory of God
John 11:1-44

"This sickness is not unto death, but for the glory of God, that the Son of God might be glorified thereby" (John 11:4). Though one may enjoy health and vitality, he may yet still be spiritually unhealthy. Likewise, a faithful man can be physically sick, as Lazarus was in Luke 16:20. When the "inner man" of a person is spiritually sick and starving, it can eventually affect that person's overall health as well. True followers of God today have help from above to "be strong," allowing them to rise to the occasion and endure misfortunes and hardships that they in turn can use to glorify God.

Meditation: In Matthew 5:16, Jesus said to let our light shine. How does the light inside of us shine outside of us?

Prayer: Lord, O God, teach us to believe in thee with our whole hearts!

Walking in the Light
John 11:10-23

"Are there not twelve hours in the day? If any man walk in the day, he stumbleth not, because he seeth the light of this world" (John 11:9). Using the example of natural light, Jesus shows that he is both *"the resurrection"* and *"the life."* He proved this when he raised his friend Lazarus back to life after he had been dead for four days. We successfully live our spiritual lives by walking in his spiritual light (1 John 1:7).

Meditation: When one obeys the Gospel then he obeys the death, burial and resurrection of Jesus Christ. How does a person do this? (See Romans 6:1-20.)

Prayer: Dear God, let us know how to obey the Gospel of thy Son Jesus Christ!

Can You Believe This?
John 11:24-35

"I am the resurrection, and the life: he that believeth in me, though he were dead, yet shall he live: And whosoever liveth and believeth in me shall never die. Believest thou this?" (John 11:25-26). It is certain that Jesus has power over life and death. We are told later

in this same chapter that he raises his good friend Lazaurus from the dead. It is evident that Jesus had great compassion for those grieving for Lazarus as he also wept. He calls for belief from those who were hearing his saving message of faith before they ever saw the miracle.

Meditation: Did Jesus cry because Lazarus died or did he cry because everyone around him was so distraught? Could it have been both?

Prayer: Lord, please show us how to turn our unbelief into belief.

Anything Is Possible
Mark 9:23; Matthew 19:26; 26:39; Mark 14:35

"If thou canst believe, all things are possible to him that believeth" (Mark 9:23). Belief in God through his Son is a pre-requisite for believing that "all things are possible". Is there anything too hard for the Lord? We are encouraged in scripture to believe that through prayer we can have what we ask for, if we ask in faith, nothing doubting, and if it is the Lord's will.

Meditation: How does a faithful prayer affect a change in the circumstances of life?

Prayer: Lord, O God, may we earnestly look for those quality moments to pray!

More than Conquerors
Mark 9:29

"This kind can come forth by nothing, but by prayer and fasting" (Mark 9:29). It's really important that Christians keep their eyes wide open. The enemy employs strongholds, traps, devises, nets, and temptations. We need consistent encouragement to resist his dark plan for us. By prayer, fasting, meditation, and study, we can gain the added determination and strength to successfully navigate through this life and fight the strongest of temptations. Jesus remains our loving advocate. Though we are not fighting demon possession today, still some temptations seem more difficult to shake than others, but God always provides us a way of escape so that we are more than conquerors through him that loves us.

Meditation: Fighting the good overall fight of faith means winning many small battles with sin. List some things you can do to better resist temptation.

Prayer: Dear Lord, I want to be more than a conqueror!

Offending a Child
Mark 9:42; Ephesians 6:1-10

"And whosoever shall offend one of these little ones that believe in me, it is better for him that a millstone were hanged about his neck, and he were cast into the

sea" (Mark 9:42). One should go to great lengths to avoid offending a young soul and hurting a soft heart. Children should all be taught the truth in love. Ephesians 6:1-3 teaches that children are to obey their parents in the Lord, and good fathers should not be delinquent in this duty, but instead, they should nurture and admonish their children in the way of righteousness.

Meditation: Why do many find it difficult to raise children to obey their parents? What does the Bible teach regarding discipline?

Prayer: Lord, may we not offend a little one.

Week 34
Little Children
Mark 10:14

"Suffer the little children to come unto me, and forbid them not: for of such is the kingdom of God" (Mark 10:14). The only way to approach God is through his Son, Jesus (John 14:6). However, small children are not yet accountable to God, because they are not mature enough to understand faith or to realize the consequences of sin. They are still innocent, pure, and guiltless. Individuals who are mature enough to be accountable to God must through faith first call upon God to be accepted (Acts 2:21, 37-38). Since every accountable person is guilty of sin (Romans 3:23), everyone needs the cleansing blood of Jesus to wash

away sins. This washing occurs within baptism according to Acts 22:16; Mark 10:15.

Meditation: Since infants are without sin, then why do some teach they must be baptized?

Prayer: Lord, let us have a pure heart as a little child!

God Is So Good!
Mark 10:18

"Why callest thou me good? There is none good but one, that is, God" (Mark 10:18). Jesus showed us how to be humble and give glory to our Father. God is so good! He deserves our best!

Meditation: If God is the source of good, who is the source of evil?

Prayer: Lord, help us to follow after only good!

One Thing Is Missing
Mark 10:21

"One thing thou lackest: go thy way, sell whatsoever thou hast, and give to the poor, and thou shalt have treasure in heaven: and come, take up the cross, and follow me" (Mark 10:21). There is often only one thing keeping us from the cross. Most of us have at least one thing that they struggle with for a lifetime; some have more than one. This young man was

hindered by his wealth. Whatever sin stands between us and God must be removed. The writer of Hebrews calls us to *"lay aside every weight, and the sin which doth so easily beset us, and let us run with patience the race that is set before us, Looking unto Jesus . . ."* (Hebrews 12:1-2). Let us not have one thing missing (Mark 10:21).

Meditation: What is a "pet sin"?

Prayer: Lord, help us to find those things that hinder us.

It is Easier for Camels
Mark 10:25

"It is easier for a camel to go through the eye of a needle, than for a rich man to enter into the kingdom of God" (Mark 10:25). It is difficult, but not impossible, for the rich to choose God's way. It is not a sin to be rich or to have possessions, but the rich often fall into many kinds of temptations because of their wealth. They may feel self-sufficient and comfortable, and they may find it difficult to focus on spiritual things, while they depend all too often on their earthly riches. Jesus told us to lay up for ourselves treasures in heaven and not on earth. (See Matthew 6:19-22.)

Meditation: Can we make things difficult on ourselves sometimes? How? Is God's way easier than man's way? Why?

Prayer: Lord, let us not allow riches to rob us.

Mission Impossible
Mark 10:27

"With men it is impossible, but not with God: for with God all things are possible" (Mark 10:27). I am weak, but he is strong! There are no problems too big for God to handle. He has never seen an unsolvable puzzle. The prophet asked if there was anything too hard for the Lord. Well, is there? There is not one situation that is too difficult for him. There is no other force or power that can rob, diminish, or relinquish him of his strength Mark 9:23.

Meditation: How does remembering the wisdom of Solomon and the strength of Samson help us see God's power more clearly?

Prayer: Lord, help us to place our confidence in thee.

Leaving Home
Mark 10:29-30

"Verily I say unto you, There is no man that hath left house, or brethren, or sisters, or father, or mother, or wife, or children, or lands, for my sake, and the gospel's, But he shall receive an hundredfold now in this time, houses, and brethren, and sisters, and mothers, and children, and lands, with persecutions; and in the world to come eternal life" (Mark 10:29-30). The Lord promises eternal life to all that leave the paths of sin and put their trust in him. Working in the Lord's business *"now in this time"* has its

challenges, but what other business plan offers so much? The benefit package and retirement option is so extraordinary that all the sacrifices, the suffering and persecution can seem merely to be small inconveniences.

Meditation: How does having trouble effect your commitments?

Prayer: Lord, help us to choose the right business plan.

They Will Spit on Him
Mark 10:33-34

"Behold, we go up to Jerusalem; and the Son of man shall be delivered unto the chief priests, and unto the scribes; and they shall condemn him to death, and shall deliver him to the Gentiles: And they shall mock him, and shall scourge him, and shall spit upon him, and shall kill him: and the third day he shall rise again" (Mark 10:33-34). Jesus here shares with his twelve apostles about his grim future, being very specific about his suffering and imminent death. But then, he lifts them from disparity and calms their troubled hearts when he tells them he will "rise again." (See John 14:1-3.)

Meditation: How important is it to be upfront and truthful with our family and friends when discussing anything?

Prayer: Lord, help us to hope in thee, O God!

Week 35

Can You Be Baptized with My Baptism?

Mark 10:38; Acts 2:38; Romans 6:1-10

"Ye know not what ye ask: can ye drink of the cup that I drink of? And be baptized with the baptism that I am baptized with?" (Mark 10:38). Jesus is probably not speaking here about his prior immersion (baptism) by John but his up-coming death on the cross, which he describes as a baptism. It's important for his disciples today to follow the example of his death, burial, and resurrection to have true salvation. With this in mind, remember that the scriptures reveal only one way to accomplish this goal—through scriptural baptism, representative of a burial with Jesus, for the remission of sins. (See Romans 6:3-7)

Meditation: Why does Jesus use his death on the cross to represent baptism? What similarities can you see?

Prayer: Lord, help us to dig deeper into thy words.

He Came to Minister

Mark 10:45

"For even the Son of man came not to be ministered unto, but to minister, and to give his life a ransom for many" (Mark 10:45). Jesus showed the servant how to serve, the leader how to lead, and the minister how

to minister. The Christian life is a giving life. We help others! We suffer for righteousness sake! We keep ourselves in the love of God!

Meditation: What lesson was Jesus teaching by washing his disciples' feet?

Prayer: Lord, help us to open our eyes to see thy will about becoming a minister to others.

Moving Mountains
Mark 11:1-33

"Have faith in God. For verily I say unto you, That whosoever shall say unto this mountain, Be thou removed, and be thou cast into the sea; and shall not doubt in his heart, but shall believe that those things which he saith shall come to pass; he shall have whatsoever he saith. Therefore I say unto you, What things soever ye desire, when ye pray, believe that ye receive them, and ye shall have them" (Mark 11:22-24). This passage is rich with the omniscience of deity. Jesus is mindful that from time to time we have lapses in faith, but he has power and providence to compensate us for our inadequacies and mercy to forgive us of every transgression. (See 1 John 1:7.)

Meditation: What is providence? Provide a working definition of it.

Prayer: Lord, help us to learn more of thee.

Become Like a Child
Matthew 18:3; John 3:1-10

"Verily I say unto you, Except ye be converted, and become as little children, ye shall not enter into the kingdom of heaven" (Matthew 18:3). Obeying the gospel and becoming a Christian causes a conversion of the mind that creates a clear conscience (1 Peter 3:21). Only then can one have a child-like heart again. Jesus told Nicodemus that except a man is "born again" he cannot see God (John 3:3, 5). Then as a Christian, one experiences a daily walk with God by the renewing of his mind as he continues to study God's word and grow in faith (Romans 12:1-5).

Meditation: What can we do to cleanse our hearts and hands?

Prayer: Lord, we hope to walk before thee with a clean heart!

Angels of Little Ones
Matthew 18:10; Proverbs 22:6; 2 Timothy 1:5

"Take heed that ye despise not one of these little ones; for I say unto you, That in heaven their angels do always behold the face of my Father which is in heaven" (Matthew 18:10). Here the Lord clearly warns against the ill-treatment of children. They are impressionable and should be encouraged rather than discouraged. A newly converted young person will need to guard against many temptations! As

adults who are concerned about where these precious souls will spend eternity, we can help them as they face perils and problems. We must set good examples for them in Bible study and prayer, as well as, how we live our faith. If they are in our immediate care, we should bring them up in the way they should go.

Meditation: What are some temptations that are especially difficult for young people?

Prayer: Lord, please be with our younger ones today.

Private Conversations
Matthew 18:15-17

"Moreover if thy brother shall trespass against thee, go and tell him his fault between thee and him alone: if he shall hear thee, thou hast gained thy brother. But if he will not hear thee, then take with thee one or two more, that in the mouth of two or three witnesses every word may be established. And if he shall neglect to hear them, tell it unto the church: but if he neglect to hear the church let him be unto thee as an heathen man and a publican" (Matthew 18:15-17). Even Christians sometimes disagree or hurt one another. Jesus emphasizes the need to work out problems between individuals within the structure of personal relationships, friends, and the church. Here we are given directions to "gain" a brother who has offended someone. It is important to point out that in the beginning, the conversations should be confidential, but if the person will not listen, then the church should get involved.

Meditation: Why do you suppose the Lord wanted to keep some matters private?

Prayer: Lord, help us to know how to restore our brethren.

Where Two or Three Are
Matthew 18:19-20

"For where two or three are gathered together in my name, there am I in the midst of them (Matthew 18:20). One of the most encouraging verses in the Bible reminds us that the Lord is interested in the faithful few. What we agree on and pray about and how we worship are all very important to him, (John 4:24). When individuals come together to pray with a single purpose in mind, the Lord is there. One of the Bible names representing Jesus is Immanuel, which means "God with us." He promises to never leave or forsake his faithful children.

Meditation: Why do you suppose the Lord wanted us to know that even if there are just a few meeting together in his name, he would accept us?

Prayer: Lord, teach us how best to achieve unity and how to keep it! Let us not be discouraged when we feel there should be more of us.

Week 36

Paying off a Credit Balance of Millions

Matthew 18:23-35; Romans 1:14-15

Jesus compares the kingdom of heaven to a certain king who wanted to look into how much he was owed by his servants. One was brought to him that owed a whopping 10,000 talents of silver (millions of dollars in modern terms). When he couldn't pay anything on his debt, the lord commanded that he, his wife, his children, and all his possessions should be sold to make a payment.

The servant fell down and asked for patience, promising to pay all that he owed. The king was moved with compassion and forgave him the entire debt. But that same servant found one that owed him 100 pence—a small amount compared to the other debt—and took him by the throat, saying, "Pay me what you owe me." This servant fell down and begged for patience, but instead the other servant had him arrested.

When the lord heard about it, he said, *"O thou wicked servant, I forgave thee all that debt . . . Shouldest not thou also have had compassion on thy fellow servant, even as I had pity on thee?"*

"So likewise shall my heavenly Father do also unto you, if ye from your hearts forgive not every one his brother their trespasses" (Matthew 18:35).

Meditation: Why is it so easy to take for granted what the Lord has done for us?

Prayer: Lord, let us be merciful!

God Made Male and Female
Matthew 19:1-6; Genesis 1:27, 5:2; Malachi 2:15

"For this cause shall a man leave father and mother, and shall cleave to his wife: and they twain shall be one flesh" (Matthew 19: 5). One of the most fundamental truths in nature is that there is both male and female. In Genesis we learn that mankind had a beginning. In Genesis 2:7, God formed man from the dust of the earth and breathed into him the breath of life. God made Adam and Eve and from this first married couple, the world was populated.

Meditation: Why would Jesus mention creating both male and female when discussing marriage?

Prayer: Lord, help us obey thy will regarding marriage.

Two Have Become One
Matthew 19:6; Matthew 5:32;
1 Corinthians 7:25-39

"Wherefore they are no more twain, but one flesh. What therefore God hath joined together, let not man put asunder" (Matthew 19:6). It is important to understand that holy matrimony is to be only

between a man and woman. No one should try to divide, separate, or take apart what the Lord has put together. It is God who joins together a husband and wife and God hates divorce; therefore, shouldn't we?

Meditation: Why are there so many divorces today? How many couples do you know today who have been married for over fifty years? Name two possible reasons for those particular couples' marriage longevity.

Prayer: Lord, O God, may we be faithful to our spouses and in doing so be a good example for others!

Only One Exception
Matthew 19:9

"And I say unto you, Whosoever shall put away his wife, except it be for fornication, and shall marry another, committeth adultery: and whoso marrieth her which is put away doth commit adultery" (Matthew 19:9). Jesus gives only one reason for divorcing his or her spouse with the Lord's approval. If someone divorces his spouse when there has been no marital unfaithfulness and then marries another, he commits adultery, and so does the one who marries the adulterer. (Read Matthew 5:31-32; Deuteronomy 24:1.)

Meditation: What kind of things could be done before and after a couple marries that would help them stay married?

195

Prayer: Lord, help us to open our eyes to see thy will.

For the Kingdom's Sake
Matthew 19:4-12

"For there are some eunuchs, which were so born from their mother's womb: and there are some eunuchs, which were made eunuchs of men: and there be eunuchs, which have made themselves eunuchs for the kingdom of heaven's sake, He that is able to receive it, let him receive it" (Matthew 19:12). Some individuals dedicate themselves so wholly to the ministry and service of God that they choose a life of celibacy. Jesus mentions this way of life in his teaching about marriage, but he never commanded celibacy as a requirement for ministers. Through his lesson we are reminded that we should find our places to serve the Lord no matter life's circumstances.

Meditation: In Acts 8, the Bible tells a story about a eunuch from Ethiopia. Do you suppose his station in life as the queen's treasurer helped or hindered his decision to obey the Lord? Could it have hindered his continued faithfulness to God?

Prayer: Lord, O God, let us honor marriage according to your teaching!

Little Children

Matthew 19:14

"Suffer little children, and forbid them not, to come unto me: for of such is the kingdom of heaven" (Matthew 19:14). On one occasion, the disciples were found ushering the small children away from Jesus. Perhaps they thought that with the crowds pressing them constantly, they needed to manage Jesus' time to allow those with more urgent matters to approach him first. Maybe they did not think that the children were in spiritual danger, so they did not need to see Jesus.

Jesus corrects them, showing the advantages of permitting the children to come to him in his ministry. Jesus placed his hands on them to bless them and often used their purity in his teachings. What parent couldn't learn from his discourse and example of compassion?

Meditation: Children offer much in the way of examples of innocence and purity. What prayers are sweeter than the prayers of a believing child?

Prayer: Lord, O God, teach us to learn purity from thee and from our children!

When Generosity Is Despised
Matthew 20:1-16

"Is it not lawful for me to do what I will with mine own? Is thine eye evil, because I am good?" (Matthew 20:15). In this parable, laborers had agreed on a penny wage. They were hired at different times of the day, at 9:00 a.m., 12:00 p.m., 3:00 p.m., and 5:00 p.m. Those hired last worked only one hour of the day, yet all received the same wage: one penny. Those who had worked longer thought they should have received more. But wasn't it up to the householder what he wanted to pay? Hadn't each agreed to accept the pay? Jealously plays a cruel game indeed when one stoops to despising the generosity of others.

Meditation: Why did the householder choose to give everyone the same? What spiritual lesson might we learn today from this story?

Prayer: Lord, O God, teach us to look at things the right way.

Week 37
My House
Matthew 21:13; Matthew 21:12-13; Isaiah 56:7

"It is written, My house shall be called the house of prayer; but ye have made it a den of thieves" (Matthew 21:13). Jesus uses the phrase "my house" to refer to the house of God, which was then the temple, but

now is called the church (1 Timothy 3:15). These people were conducting business and were upbraided because they had begun buying and selling in a holy place, thereby defiling it. What they were doing was not necessarily wrong, but where they were doing it was sinful and it greatly angered Jesus.

Meditation: Name some ways that places of worship could be misused today?

Prayer: Lord, teach us to know how to behave in the house of God, the church of the living God.

Perfect Praise
Matthew 21:16; Matthew 21:14-16; Psalms 8:2

"Yea; have ye never read, Out of the mouth of babes and sucklings thou hast perfected praise?" (Matthew 21:16).

"Yes, The Scriptures say, 'You have taught children and babes to give praise.' Have you not read that Scripture?" (Matthew 21:16 ERV).

These children were chanting "Hosanna to the son of David." Often times, children are the ones unafraid to praise the Lord and confess before others their faith in him. They seldom seem ashamed or afraid of embarrassment or persecution.

Meditation: Why were only the children crying out these words and not the adults? What might that say about church members of our congregations today?

Prayer: Lord, teach us not to be ashamed of thee and thy word!

Be Fruitful
Matthew 21:19

"Let no fruit grow on thee henceforward forever" (Matthew 21:19). The Lord throughout his brief ministry showed us how to be patient in suffering. This virtue is certainly needed to produce good fruit; however, we are not promised a tomorrow. Time is short, and there will come a time when unfruitful trees will be taken away. Until then, God's children are to continue to grow and produce good fruit. Jesus said in his great sermon on the mountain that corrupt trees cannot produce good fruit and that every tree that doesn't produce good fruit will be cut down and cast into the fire. (See Matthew 7:16-20.)

Meditation: Why do people procrastinate when it comes to doing spiritual things for God?

Prayer: Lord, help us to put off the old man and put on the new man.

Prayer Power
Matthew 21:21-22

"Verily I say unto you, If ye have faith, and doubt not, ye shall not only do this which is done to the fig tree, but also if ye shall say unto this mountain, Be thou removed, and be thou cast into the sea; it shall be done.

And all things, whatsoever ye shall ask in prayer, believing, ye shall receive" (Matthew 21:21-22). Great things can be accomplished when we believe that what we pray about can happen. Mountains can be moved today when one prays with a shovel in his hand. Prayers go unanswered when one doubts God's power. He can do so much more than we can possibly imagine, but we must be willing to roll up our sleeves and be ready to do our part.

Meditation: Do you believe Jesus meant moving an actual mountain? Was he speaking of only a miraculous event?

Prayer: Lord, O God! Let us not doubt when we pray!

Jesus Refuses to Answer
Matthew 21:24-27

"I also will ask you one thing, which if ye tell me, I in likewise will tell you by what authority I do these things. The baptism of John, whence was it? From heaven, or of men?" (Matthew 21:24-25). Jesus, realizing that he was being set up, wisely turns the table upon his invokers and invites them to first answer his question. The correct answer to his question would give them the answer they were seeking for their question. But the chief priests and elders, as usual, had difficulty in providing an answer; they knew that either answer would incriminate themselves!

Meditation: Can you find another instance where Jesus answered a question with a question?

Prayer: Lord, help us to know how to answer when others ask us about our faith.

I Go, Sir!
Matthew 21:28-32

"Verily I say unto you, That the publicans and the harlots go into the kingdom of God before you" (Matthew 21:31). The tax collectors and harlots had terrible reputations in Christ's day, yet Jesus said they were ready to embrace the gospel amidst all persecution and "going into the kingdom" before others. Why? They were willing to repent! Their courage was probably a result of making some restitution for their past behavior. They had put off their "old selves" and put on Christ Jesus through repentance and obedience. Thus when converting to Christianity, they made Jesus their Lord and Savior and God their spiritual Father. (See Matthew 21:28-31; Matthew 7:21.)

Meditation: Why would sinners embrace Christianity more than would religious people?

Prayer: Lord, help us be ashamed of our past sins and get on board to behave better!

He Sent His Son
Matthew 21:33-40

"But last of all he sent unto them his son, saying, They will reverence my son" (Matthew 21:37). This parable illustrates that some will know and respect Jesus as both Lord and King, but unfortunately, others will not. Jesus says "last of all" the son was sent. Do you see a fulfillment or an end to the Lord's merciful patience in this statement?

Meditation: Read this story slowly and think about its implications.

Prayer: Lord, help us to both read and study the truth.

Week 38
Head of the Corner
Matthew 21:42

"Did ye never read in the scriptures, The stone which the builders rejected, the same is become the head of the corner: this is the Lord's doing, and it is marvelous in our eyes?" (Matthew 21:42). The stone obviously refers to Jesus Christ. Throughout biblical history, he is called the chief corner stone as a reference to his authority and position as head of the body, his church. Unfortunately, the chief cornerstone is still rejected by many today. Many have spearheaded

their own churches without his approval, thereby sidestepping and rejecting his authority. Believers should beware of becoming members of any *"body"* (church) that does not wear the name of Christ or does not uphold the doctrine or teachings of Christ. (See Matthew 21:42-46.)

Meditation: How many kinds of bodies of Christ are mentioned in the New Testament?

Prayer: Lord, may we only seek thee, the true and living God!

Gentiles Have Faith, Too
Matthew 21:42-46

"Therefore say I unto you, The kingdom of God shall be taken from you, and given to a nation bringing forth the fruits thereof" (Matthew 21:43). Jesus saw a time that the Gentile nation would be more receptive to the gospel than his own Jewish nation. The church was established in Acts 2 when about 3,000 Jews were baptized. About ten years after Pentecost, the first recorded Gentiles converted to Christianity. Cornelius and his family and friends all became Christians after they had heard the saving message of the gospel and were commanded to be baptized in Acts 10:48. As the book of Acts unfolds, there are many conversions of both the Jews and Gentiles.

Meditation: What does Matthew 21:43 imply today when Christians stop bearing fruit?

Prayer: Lord, help us to bear fruit for Thee!

100 Sheep
Luke 15:3-6

"What man of you, having an hundred sheep, if he lose one of them, doth not leave the ninety and nine in the wilderness, and go after that which is lost, until he find it?" (Luke 15:4). Seeking the lost is what Jesus came to do. All of God's children today are expected to "be about our Father's business" as Jesus was (Luke 2:49). We find that regathering those who have wandered away is an enormous task for a shepherd. It goes without saying that the "99" who remain faithful should not require constant attention, particularly during such a time as when there are those who require special attention.

Meditation: Would it be correct to say that every person alive today will fit into one of the two following groups: either a lost sheep or a saved one? Must the Savior expect his shepherds to search constantly after us when we are already found?

Prayer: Lord, help us to remain in the fold of safety!

Ten Silver Coins
Luke 15:8-10

"Either what woman having ten pieces of silver, if she lose one piece, doth not light a candle, and sweep the house, and seek diligently till she find it?" (Luke 15:8). Placing proper value on souls sometimes requires us to make a comparison to something we commonly value. The woman mentioned above takes three

painstaking steps to find her silver: lighting a candle, sweeping her house, and seeking diligently. This analogy shows us just how incredibly valuable a soul is to our Lord!

Meditation: Does Jesus imply through the analogy that one should never stop looking for a silver coin?

Prayer: O God, help us to see the value you place on just one soul.

I Have Sinned
Luke 15:11-32

"I will arise and go to my father, and will say unto him, Father, I have sinned against heaven, and before thee, And am no more worthy to be called thy son: make me as one of thy hired servants" (Luke 15:18-19). The wayward son came first to the one person who could help him the most: he first "came to himself." We need humility to admit our mistakes; then we need a renewed determination to choose the right path to heaven. So it is important that we look deep inside ourselves and find commitment.

Leaving home for the first time is very difficult for most young people. The world is no place for someone who has not made up his or her mind to be strong. Sin has a way of grabbing us, and it does not want to let go. When we recognize sin in our lives, we must quickly admit it and turn from it. The best thing to do with a guilty conscience is to confess the wrong and seek forgiveness.

Meditation: Is it better to think less of one's self-worth or more?

Prayer: Lord, help us not to focus too much on ourselves!

Wasting Time
Luke 16:1-12

"And the Lord commended the unjust steward, because he had done wisely: for the children of this world are in their generation wiser than the children of light" (Luke 16:8). Good stewards learn to be prudent and faithful with all that is entrusted to them, especially with regard to their personal time. The steward in this parable begins to reduce all of the debt of his employer's creditors. Though he had been unjust in the past, this made him a hero in their eyes. It is important for every Christian to be proactive and careful with stewardship, so that we don't swerve from our path to heaven. If we squander our precious moments, talents, and other gifts that have been given to us, we will bring to ourselves heartache; and to God, we will bring disappointment. The choice is clear.

Meditation: What does this story teach regarding making amends for our actions?

Prayer: O God, let us count each precious moment.

Faithful With a Little
Luke 16:10-13; 1 Corinthians 16:1-5

"He that is faithful in that which is least is faithful also in much: and he that is unjust in the least is unjust also in much" (Luke 16:10). Faithful stewardship towards God is required by every one of his children. Faithfulness in general is a lifetime commitment until the time when we lay our crosses down and enter into the next life (Revelation 2:10).

Meditation: List five areas in which we might improve our stewardship.

Prayer: Lord, help us to have a lifetime commitment.

Week 39

The Love of Money
Luke 16:1-12

"No servant can serve two masters: for either he will hate the one and love the other; or else he will hold to the one, and despise the other. Ye cannot serve God and mammon" (Luke 16:13). We can use money to love and serve others. However, when we begin to love and serve money, we also begin to use and manipulate people—a sure sign of a serious spiritual problem. Attempting to serve two masters will always end with serving only one.

Meditation: Is money evil? Is it good? How can we detect the love of money in our lives?

Prayer: Lord God, teach us to choose to serve thee!

Justifying One's Self
Luke 16:15

"Ye are they which justify yourselves before men; but God knoweth your hearts: for that which is highly esteemed among men is abomination in the sight of God" (Luke 16:15). The attempt to justify one's self in the presence of others is very common, but to seek God's approval is to leave "self" out of it. A Christian must deny himself to be a true follower of the Lord.

Meditation: Why must a person deny himself while carrying his cross?

Prayer: Lord God, teach us to deny ourselves.

Church = Kingdom
Luke 16:16

"The law and the prophets were until John: since that time the kingdom of God is preached, and every man presseth into it" (Luke 16:16). The kingdom of God began to be preached during John's ministry. The message was simply that the church of Christ would soon be established, fulfilling God's plan to redeem man. Some have mistakenly commented that, since Jesus said men were "pressing into it," the church must have begun in the days of John with John as a great church leader. However, John's job was to announce the coming of Jesus, the Messiah, not to

establish the church. In Matthew 16:18, Jesus promises to build his church, which we know took place on the Day of Pentecost after Christ was resurrected and had ascended to heaven (Acts 1 and 2). Prior to this time, men were baptized with John's baptism. The faithful under the Law of Moses and in the Patriarchal Age were also incapable of Jesus' baptism prior to his perfect sacrifice, but they would receive atonement once Jesus went to the cross. When Jesus' blood was finally shed at Calvary, all would receive the potential for remission of sins. This gift of salvation is for every obedient follower. (See Luke 16:16.)

Meditation: What did Jesus mean when he said everyone was pressing into the kingdom?

Prayer: Lord, give us zeal to fight the good fight.

Lazarus and the Rich Man
Luke 16:19-31

"But Abraham said, Son, remember that thou in thy lifetime received thy good things, and likewise Lazarus evil things: but now he is comforted, and thou are tormented" (Luke 16:25). Within this brief biography of two men, one is interested in the pleasures of life, while the other is interested in the things of God. This poignant story reminds us that we should not expect a comfortable eternal afterlife, if while living comfortably in this life, we are not paying attention to the Lord's desired plan for each of us. The proper focus for true believers is always first the kingdom of God and his righteousness (Matthew 6:33). No one

today is promised health and wealth. Even poor Lazarus did not have many of those things that would have made his life comfortable in his later years. But because of his faithfulness to the Lord, he now possesses true riches that last forever.

Meditation: What might this story teach us about the brevity of life?

Prayer: Lord, help us to see that our days on the Earth are few. Let us hold on to those precious moments and make the best of them.

Doing Our Duty
Luke 17:7-10

"So likewise ye, when ye shall have done all those things which are commanded you, say, We are unprofitable servants: we have done that which was our duty to do" (Luke 17:10). Some people seem to expect an extra measure of thanks or money from their employers simply for doing their job. Christians are commanded to fulfill their duties with a sense of humility and honorable perspective and for no other reason than that they love the Lord and desire heaven to be their home. In other words, we should never feel like our work is good enough to earn us a place in heaven, though we are told to maintain good works. This implies that we should always go the extra mile.

Meditation: How will we know where the first mile ends and the extra mile begins?

Prayer: Lord, let us not be too lazy to go the second mile.

Where Are the Nine?
Luke 17:12-19

"Were there not ten cleansed? but where are the nine?" (Luke 17:17). This story of compassion helps to remind us how important it is to be thankful for what the Lord has done for us. In this reading, only one returns and is thankful, which highlights the fact that this lack of appreciation could be true of many today. To be grateful for the blessings we receive daily gives God the glory.

Meditation: What does counting our blessings do for us?

Prayer: Lord, O God, help us to count our blessings and be grateful!

A Spiritual Kingdom
Luke 17:20-22

"The kingdom of God cometh not with observation: Neither shall they say, Lo here! Or, lo there! For, behold, the kingdom of God is within you" (Luke 17:20-21 KJV).
"The kingdom of God is not coming with signs to be observed, nor will they say, Look, here it is! Or There! For behold the kingdom of God is in the midst of you" (Luke 17:20-21 ERV).

The kingdom of God today is a spiritual kingdom. Many in Jesus' day were looking for a sign. Their misunderstanding centered around the thought that the kingdom of God would be a physical kingdom and would be physically fixed and visible upon the earth in literal Jerusalem. Some are still looking for a literal or earthly kind of kingdom today. These millennialists or pre-millennialists prefer to believe that the Lord still has a plan to set up his kingdom on earth. But establishing his spiritual, not physical kingdom, is exactly what he already came to earth to do, and he succeeded! King Jesus is now reigning!

Meditation: What are some differences between a spiritual and physical kingdom?

Prayer: Lord, thank you for finding room for me in thy kingdom!

Week 40
Just like Lightning
Luke 17:24

"For the lightning, that lighteneth out of the one part under heaven, shineth unto the other part under heaven; so shall also the Son of man be in his day" (Luke 17:24). Jesus explains that the destruction of Jerusalem would be very visible, not hidden, just like lightening that lights the sky. The use of this language brings to mind the visible nature of Jesus' return. The words "for every eye shall see him" (Revelation 1:7) show us the magnitude of his return. The second coming of Jesus Christ will be a global event, just as

was the flood in the days of Noah. When the Lord returns it will be day in one time zone and night in another, yet every eye will see him.

Meditation: Have you ever considered the sounds that the eight heard while inside the ark during the 40 days and nights? What did the rainbow represent?

Prayer: Lord, O God, may we all be ready for that last day!

The Flood Came
Luke 17: 26-27

"They did eat, they drank, they married wives, they were given in marriage, until the day that Noah entered into the ark, and the flood came, and destroyed them all" (Luke 17:27). There were no apparent warning signs in Noah's day before the rain and flood came. This is why normal every day activities were not postponed. The huge ark itself, along with the preaching of Noah, should have been enough to persuade someone to save himself from the deluge. The fact that Noah and his family of eight were the only survivors is used as an example in the New Testament. In 1 Peter 3:21, Peter uses the phrase *"the like figure"* to show that Noah's salvation from the flood is like people's salvation from sin today, a salvation accomplished through baptism via full immersion in water. Peter continues to explain the likeness: "wherein baptism does now also save us." This great worldwide event gives us a glimpse of the end of time itself, to that final day: the Day of

Judgment. At that time, the world will be destroyed again, not with water, but with fire.

Meditation: What warning did the people in Noah's day have of the impending flood? What warnings do we have today regarding the judgment day?

Prayer: Lord, O God, help us notice the warning signs even when they are not apparent.

Lot's Wife
Luke 17:31-32; Genesis 19

"Remember Lot's wife" (Luke 17:32). Many examples of warnings from the Old Testament appear in the New Testament. One of them, *"Remember Lot's wife"* is a reference to the story of Lot and his family who left Sodom and Gomorrah just before God overthrew the two cities. Though they were warned not to look back, Lot's wife did so to her detriment (Genesis 19:15-17, 25-26). As Christians, we may be tempted to return to sinful habits we practiced before we knew the Lord. Remembering Lot's wife is a warning of the dangers we will face if we return to sin after beginning our walk with Christ.

Meditation: Why did Lot's wife look back? What might cause us to look back at our former life, though we now walk with the Lord?

Prayer: Lord, help us to open our eyes to see thy will.

Where Eagles Gather
Luke 17:35-40

"Wheresoever the body is, thither will the eagles be gathered together" (Luke 17:37). Some commentators believe that the "eagles" mentioned here were angels, a reference to the spirit leaving the body and returning to the one who gave it. Others argue that they describe the armies that would destroy Jerusalem in A. D. 70, since the Romans used images of eagles to represent their power and dominion within their empire. Whichever explanation one adopts, he can know the Lord is certainly in charge of the future and that the righteous can have assurance that he has our best interest at heart.

Meditation: Are there any scriptures that describe angels as eagles? Are some angels described as having wings? Do all angels have wings?

Prayer: Lord, O God, may we always be ready for the Judgement Day!

Leave Her Alone
John 12:1-8; 1 Corinthians 15:50

"Let her alone: against the day of my burying hath she kept this. For the poor always ye have with you; but me ye have not always" (John 12:7-8). The disciples would not always have Jesus in human form. He would soon experience a cruel death on a cross. He

would be buried and rise after three days from the dead early on Sunday morning. Jesus reportedly told his disciples that they would always have him in spirit, for he had said, *"I will never leave thee, nor forsake thee"* (Hebrews 13:5).

Meditation: When Jesus told his disciples to leave this woman alone, what did he want them not to do?

Prayer: Lord, help us to trust that you are near.

A New Life
John 12:24-25

"Verily, verily, I say unto you, Except a corn of wheat fall into the ground and die, it abideth alone: but if it die, it bringeth forth much fruit. He that loveth his life shall lose it; and he that hateth his life in this world shall keep it unto life eternal." (John 12:24-25). This is likely a passage parallel in meaning to John 3:1-5: *"Except a man be born again, he cannot see God."* In this important process of one's salvation, the old life is put away as the new life emerges. The Christian life is described in scripture as a new beginning.

Meditation: If there emerges a new man in our conversion then what happens to the old man?

Prayer: Dear God, thank you for our new life!

Father, Save Me
John 12:27; 1 Corinthians 10:13; 1 Peter 4:16

"Now is my soul troubled; and what shall I say? Father, save me from this hour: but for this cause came I unto this hour. Father, glorify thy name" (John 12:27-28). Each Christian is destined to suffer to some degree. Persecutions and trouble will follow God's children – all of us – as we follow Jesus. However, the Father promised he would never allow us to be tempted above what we are able to endure. Glory to God!

Meditation: If Jesus knew he would die from crucifixion why did he say, "save me from this hour"?

Prayer: Lord, help us in our hour of temptation.

Week 41

Lifting up Jesus
John 12:32-33

"And I, if I be lifted up from the earth, will draw all men unto me" (John 12:32). The "lifted up" Christ is a power drawing the souls of men. The above verse is likely a reference to Moses lifting up the brass serpent in the wilderness, a means by which the people could be healed of their infirmities and escape death. The worst disease known to man is the sickening disease called sin, but the Great Physician has the remedy. He was lifted up on the cross to die for our sins. (See Numbers 21:5-9.)

Meditation: What would happen when those who had been snake bitten did not look towards the brass serpent?

Prayer: Lord, help us to always look unto thee.

Judged by the Word
John 12:48; 1 Timothy 4:13; 2 Timothy 2:15

"He that rejecteth me, and receiveth not my words, hath one that judgeth him: the word that I have spoken, the same shall judge him in the last day" (John 12:48). We must all receive Jesus and his words if we expect to be saved. It is what we need most to both live by and to die by; and it is what everyone will be judged by on that great day of judgement. Jesus said in John 17:17 that God's word is truth. It is through truth that men and women are sanctified and prepared for the Master's use.

Meditation: By rejecting the teaching of Christ, is someone also rejecting Christ himself? Please explain.

Prayer: Lord, help us and have mercy on us.

Washing Feet
John 13:12-15; 1 Timothy 5:10

"Know ye what I have done to you? Ye call me Master and Lord: and ye say well; for so I am. If I then, your Lord and Master, have washed your feet; ye also ought

to wash one another's feet. For I have given you an example, that ye should do as I have done to you" (John 13: 12-15). By washing their feet, the Lord shows his disciples the meaning of humility and service, and he commissions them to go and do likewise. Some have mistakenly commented that Jesus was commanding them to add the practice of washing feet to their ministry and worship, but he was merely showing them an example of how to love and to serve one another.

Meditation: The New Testament records examples of singing, praying, giving, preaching, and taking the Lord's Supper as acts of worship. Can you find examples of washing feet as an act of worship?

Prayer: Lord, let us know thy commands as we read your word!

A New Commandment
John 13:34-35; Colossians 2:14

"A new commandment I give unto you, That ye love one another; as I have loved you, that ye also love one another. By this shall all men know that ye are my disciples, if ye have love one to another" (John 13:34-35). All of the commandments of the New Testament are described as new. All of the commandments of the Old Testament, including the Ten Commandments, are described as old. These old laws were all nailed to the cross, where the old covenant was fulfilled or made complete. Some examples of Old Testament practices include circumcision, keeping the Sabbath, instrumental

worship, and animal sacrifices. Love is the motivating force behind keeping the new law and is how faith works. The Old Testament was full of outward practices. The New Testament (law) is the one of inward transformation that results in good works for God's glory.

Meditation: Which Old Testament practices do some want to still observe today?

Prayer: Lord, help us to rightly divide thy word.

A Rooster Crows
John 13:38; Matthew 26: 69-75; John 21:15-17

"Wilt thou lay down thy life for my sake? Verily, verily, I say unto thee, The cock shall not crow, till thou hast denied me thrice" (John 13:38). Peter, one of Christ's closest friends and apostles, offered to die with him. Each disciple of Christ today should be willing to make this same sacrifice. Later, that same night, despite his promise to the contrary, Peter denied knowing Christ. In so doing, he avoided certain arrest and possible death. Fortunately, Peter was so sorry for his weakness that he repented of this wrong and afterward prepared himself for his Master's use. About two months later, he preached to an audience of tens of thousands on the day of Pentecost (Acts 2:37-38).

Meditation: When Jesus later asked Peter three times if Peter loved him John 21:15-17, do you think it was possibly because Peter had also denied him three times Luke 22:61?

Prayer: Lord, O God, teach us to love thee more than we love even our own lives!

Mansions
John 14:1-5

"In my Father's house are many mansions: if it were not so, I would have told you. I go to prepare a place for you" (John 14:2). This world is not our permanent home. Every faithful child of God has been promised a place in heaven: a room, a house, a mansion. As Jesus went to prepare that place for us, we are also to make preparations. We are to lay up for ourselves riches in heaven instead of only gathering treasures for our life here upon the earth. (Read Matthew 6:19-21.)

Meditation: Do the many rooms or mansions in Jesus' statement portray that many people will enter into glory?

Prayer: Lord, O God, teach us to be prepared for the place prepared for us.

Jesus is the Way
John 14:6

"I am the way, the truth, and the life; no man cometh unto the Father, but by me" (John 14:6). Jesus has God's "phone number." Since there is only one Christ, "the way" in this passage is singular; the article "the" denotes a singular way, a singular "truth," and a

singular "life." The meaning is simple: without Jesus Christ, we cannot have any of these things. No one knows the way to the kingdom of heaven without having first called (dialed in), obeyed, and walked on his highway. Jesus holds the treasure map, and only Jesus knows the way to eternal life; each must follow him to arrive there eventually.

Meditation: How did Jesus answer Thomas's question?

Prayer: Lord, O God, teach us thy perfect truth!

Week 42
Jesus Looks like God
John 14:9, 22; Matthew 5:16

"Have I been so long time with you, and yet hast thou not known me, Philip? He that hath seen me hath seen the Father; and how sayest thou then, Show us the Father?" (John 14:9). Every faithful child of God today should be showing the Father to others (Matthew 5:16). In Christ's day, those who looked on Jesus with their own eyes could actually say they saw God. Christ also once told his disciples that he was the "express image" of his Father. Even so, it is always more important for his followers to know how he lived, always pleasing his Father, than to know how he looked while in the flesh. (See John 14:22.)

Meditation: Since Jesus had no earthly birth father, from whom did he receive his physical attributes and features?

Prayer: Lord, O God, teach us to open our spiritual eyes and look to thee!

Do You Love Me?
John 14:15; James 2:14-26

"If you love me, keep my commandments" (John 14:15). Loving the Lord today means obeying and keeping the New Testament commandments. Some claim contributing to our own salvation dispels grace and diminishes faith in the Lord's ability to save without the work of men. On the contrary, men were created to be workers of good works. It is by these that we glorify God and show others that we are his servants (Matthew 5:16). Good works serve both to deepen the Lord's grace and to show our love for him. There are different kinds of works. Works of vainglory will not get us to the Promised Land, but faith-focused, non-meritorious works done without regard for recognition from others is rewarded by God. Faith without works is dead (James 2:26).

Meditation: Is "grace only" faith as detrimental to Christian productivity and diligence as "works only" faith?

Prayer: Lord, O God, teach us how to first save ourselves so that we may save others!

Keep My Words
John 14:23

"If a man love me, he will keep my words: and my Father will love him, and we will come unto him, and make our abode with him" (John 14:23). The Christian has both the Father and Son's presence through Jesus and the Holy Spirit. Keeping God's "words" means obeying the Lord and showing a Christian's love of God. (See John 14:15.)

Meditation: Why do people usually keep personal letters they've received from those they love? How is that like keeping God's word close?

Prayer: Lord, O God, may we keep the faith as we share it with others!

Don't Be Afraid
John 14:27

"Peace I leave with you, my peace I give unto you: not as the world giveth, give I unto you. Let not your heart be troubled, neither let it be afraid" (John 14:27). It takes the right kind of peace to be unafraid. The peace that Jesus offers far exceeds the false peace promised by anyone else. It guards the minds and hearts of Christians while hope anchors the soul. Who can put a price on having a good conscience, peace of mind, and a fearless heart? (See Hebrew 13:5.)

Meditation: What does "being content" really mean? Are all kinds of fear destructive?

Prayer: Lord, O God, teach us the way to have peace everlasting!

My Father is Greater
John 14: 28

"Ye have heard how I said unto you, I go away, and come again unto you. If ye loved me, ye would rejoice, because I said, I go unto the Father: for my Father is greater than I" (John 14:28). As Jesus nears the time of his departure from the earth, he shows his great humility by telling his disciples that his Father is greater than himself and that they would see him briefly afterwards, (after his resurrection), before He ascended.

If the general populace of all Judeo-Christian religions would accept this one particular truth (humility), there would be a phenomenal mass rush to accept the Savior and all of his teachings. Unification of such magnitude would be dynamic and vital to world salvation. Just as pride eventually causes us much heartache, humility eventually exalts us, and ignorance is the downfall in any nation (James 1:12-14).

Meditation: What could Jesus have meant when he said, "My Father is greater than I"?

Prayer: Lord, teach us to submit fully to thy will!

The Wedding
Matthew 22:1-10

"The kingdom of heaven is like a certain king [who] sent forth his servants to call them that were bidden to the wedding: and they would not come" (Matthew 22:2-3). Jesus uses a wedding invitation to show us that there is an open invitation for salvation to all. Some have gladly accepted, while others are not planning to attend just as in the example of the wedding. Of those who did arrive, some stepped out for a while. They are those who have had their sins washed away by the blood of the Lamb, but abandoned Christ and returned to their former lives. However, the goodness of God can lead them again to repentance; with time and opportunity, deserters can once more turn to the Lord in faith and be restored to their eternal inheritance.

Meditation: Why did the Lord use a wedding to illustrate his gospel message?

Prayer: Lord, O God, let us always be ready to meet the Bridegroom when he arrives.

Few are Chosen
Matthew 22:10-14

"For many are called, but few are chosen." (Matthew 22:14). Jesus said many will choose the wrong way but a few will find the straight and narrow path that leads to eternal life. Will you be among them?

Meditation: Why do you suppose the Lord revealed to us that few will be saved and many lost? What is the difference in a straight gate and a wide gate?

Prayer: Lord, O God, teach us to love and reach out to the lost even more!

Week 43

Paying Taxes

Matthew 22:21; Matthew 22:10-14; 2 Corinthians 9:7

"Render therefore unto Caesar the things which are Caesar's; and unto God the things that are God's" (Matthew 22:21). Throughout history, taxes have been imposed to collect revenue to fund governments, and Jesus told his followers to obey the law and pay taxes. There are many benefits that we enjoy from both federal and state treasuries. For the Christian, paying taxes (giving to Caesar what belongs to him) is usually the right thing to do. We should also give to God the things that are his. We are to "lay by in store" every first day of the week and give to God cheerfully and purposefully (1 Corinthians 16:1-2).

Meditation: If people can't feel good about their giving, are they justified in not giving at all?

Prayer: Lord, O God, teach us to give cheerfully and selflessly.

Angels Do not Marry
Matthew 22:29-33

"For in the resurrection they neither marry, nor are given in marriage, but are as the angels of God in heaven" (Matthew 22:30). Angelic beings do not marry, nor are they given in marriage. For all those who reach heaven, physical relationships will give way to spiritual ones. This means that all the pain, weaknesses, and frailties of our human selves will be changed into a glorious body. All the joy and pleasures we think we have now in the flesh will not compare with those that await us there. (This is why the erroneous interpretation given by some, for Genesis 6:2, that there were giants on the earth due to the intermarriage of angels with earthly women is more than a gross exaggeration.)

Meditation: How might we be like angels in other areas? How do angels minister to us?

Prayer: Lord, O God, thank thee for all thy angels who minister unto us!

Love the Lord
Matthew 22: 36-39

"Thou shalt love the Lord thy God with all thy heart, and with all thy soul, and with all thy mind. This is the first and great commandment. And the second is like unto it, thou shalt love thy neighbor as thyself" (Matthew 22:36-39). When a people love God with their whole being, a whole new world opens up for

them. Upon these two commandments hinges (hangs) all others!

Meditation: Once, someone asked Jesus, "And who is my neighbor?" Who asked this question and how did Jesus respond? Give a reference.

Prayer: Lord, O God, may our love principally grow for thee and subsequently grow for others!

David Calls Him Lord
Matthew 22:41-45

"If David then called him Lord, how is he his son?" (Matthew 22:45). David's genealogy includes Christ as his offspring, but in the Lord's family, David is instead his child. In human terms, Jesus is a descendent or son of David. In spiritual terms, David is a child of Christ. How then can people today be related to Christ?

All who "put the Lord on" in baptism and become a part of the family of God have Christ as their Lord and Savior! (See Galatians 3:27.)

Meditation: How did his listeners respond to the question above? How would you have answered it?

Prayer: Lord, O God, teach us how to become children of God!

Call No Man Father
Matthew 23:1-10

"And call no man your father upon the earth: for one is your Father, which is in heaven" (Matthew 23:9). Christians today have only one spiritual Father. Jesus warned against sharing names meant for God with mortals in a spiritual or religious sense. He did not forbid us to call our earthly male parent "father." However, he wants us to respect how holy he is compared to sinful man. Here are some of the names in scripture that shouldn't become religious epitaphs: "Reverend," "Lord," "Master," "Ruler," and "Potentate."

Meditation: What are some of the ways we know that God is a jealous God? Why should people never use "Reverend" to refer to religious leaders?

Prayer: Lord, O God, teach us to revere only thy name!

Be a Real Christian
Matthew 23:28-33

"Even so ye also outwardly appear righteous unto men, but within ye are full of hypocrisy . . ." (Matthew 23:28). True Christianity is an "inside-and-outside" religion. Every disciple of Christ longs to have a pure heart, as well as, clean hands. To become a real Christian, one must properly call upon the name of the Lord (Acts 2:21), and then obey the instructive answer to the question found Acts 2:37-38.

Meditation: If the crowd at Pentecost knew that calling on the name of the Lord was just a matter of public confession and affirmation, why did they ask how to do so in Acts 2:37?

Prayer: Lord, O God, teach us to know what true Christianity is!

Gathering Chickens
Matthew 23: 34-39

"O Jerusalem, Jerusalem, thou that killest the prophets, and stonest them which are sent unto thee, how often would I have gathered thy children together, even as a hen gathereth her chickens under her wings, and ye would not!" (Matthew 23:37). The Lord's desire was for his people – the people of Israel – to be saved. Eventually, the Gentile nations would be included as the Lord's people, when they turned to the Lord in obedience. *"But in every nation he that feareth him, and worketh righteousness, is accepted with him"* (Acts10:35). Everyone, regardless of race, would realize that becoming a true child of God is a matter of faithful obedience, not genealogy. The Lord taught unity for all of his followers, yet even today, some refuse to be unified, allowing many diverse doctrines to both confuse and divide. (See James 2:26)

Meditation: Why did some people desire to kill and stone to death prophets of God? Shouldn't they have been afraid to do so?

Prayer: Lord, O God, admonish us into unity among all thy believers!

Week 44
Simply Marvelous
Mark 12:1-11

"And have ye not read this scripture; The stone which the builders rejected is become the head of the corner: This was the Lord's doing, and it is marvelous in our eyes?" (Mark 12:10-11). Both Christ and his church were rejected by many in the first century. Judaism, Herodism, and other sects were prevalent, causing unbelief and disrupting truth and unity. But for his apostles and ministers, it was business as usual. Miracles were diminishing, and would soon stop when the Revelation of John was complete and when John and others who had these gifts were gone. Although miracles have ceased, marvelous things are still being accomplished today through the gospel of his ministry, prayer, and providence!

Meditation: Do those who believe that miracles are still being performed today also believe that people are being raised from the dead? Are there good reasons to believe that miracles performed by men have stopped? What are some of those reasons?

Prayer: Lord, O God, teach us to rightly divine thy word!

Almost Persuaded
Mark 12:28-34

"Thou art not far from the kingdom of God" (Mark 12:34). Some individuals are closer to salvation than others; however, the Lord desires everyone to know the truth and come to him. Being close to salvation will not be enough at the judgment (Matthew 7:21). Remember what Paul said to King Agrippa who, after hearing the truth, stated that he was almost persuaded to become a Christian. *"I would to God, that not only thou, but also all that hear me this day, were both almost, and altogether such as I am, except these bonds"* (Acts 26:29).

Meditation: Do you believe there are many who are "almost persuaded" to become Christians today? What do you think is keeping them from being fully persuaded?

Prayer: Lord, O God, teach us to be able to persuade others to obey thee!

Son of David
Mark 12: 35-40

"How say the scribes that Christ is the Son of David?" (Mark 12:35). On this occasion, Jesus asks a question while teaching in the temple. It isn't surprising that no one could answer Jesus' question after they made such an assumption. Then Jesus says to beware of the scribes, for they *"love to go in long clothing, and love salutations in the marketplaces, and the chief*

seats in the synagogues" (Mark 12:38-39). These same individuals also loved the uppermost rooms at the feasts, and they prayed long prayers for show.

Meditation: Why couldn't the scribes answer Jesus question? What is the answer to it?

Prayer: Dear God, let us study to show ourselves approved unto thee, and study also that we may be able to answer important questions asked by others!

No Stone Upon Another
Mark 13:1-11

"Seest thou these great buildings? There shall not be left one stone upon another that shall not be thrown down" (Mark 13:2). Jesus revealed that the great massive stones of the temple would be cast down. Since the Lord knew Jerusalem would fall in the near future, he warned his disciples not to trust in physical things; they are not permanent. We can learn from this great city's demise that the world and everything that seems permanent to us will be destroyed one day. More importantly, our future security rests in the Lord's promises and in our home above, not in earthly temples or cities.

Meditation: The church is characterized as being built up stone upon stone with Jesus as the chief corner stone. With this in mind, what could the "tearing down" of the temple represent in a spiritual sense?

Prayer: Lord, O God, may we do what we can to edify the members of Christ's true church!

When Love Grows Cold
Matthew 24: 4-14

"And because iniquity shall abound, the love of many shall wax cold" (Matthew 24:12). It is certain that when we see apostasy and hypocrisy growing in our society, we may grow weary of well doing. We can guard against this, however, with daily prayer, godly devotion, diligent faith, and steadfast hope (Hebrews 11:6).

Meditation: What does Peter write about in 1 Peter chapter 3 that can help Christians to remain faithful?

Prayer: Lord, O God, let us be faithful to thee unto death!

Angels Are Coming
Matthew 24:31

"And he shall send his angels with a great sound of a trumpet, and they shall gather together his elect from the four winds, from one end of heaven to the other" (Matthew 24:31). The prophesied destruction of Jerusalem, which occurred in A.D. 70, included safety for every faithful follower of Christ. The destruction would serve as an effective prelude to the destruction of the earthly world alongside the "gathering of the saints" at the end of time. Please study this entire

chapter 24 to determine where Jesus ends his discussion about Jerusalem and begins to address his answer about the end of all things.

Meditation: Since angels are "ministering spirits," Hebrews 1:14, what do they do for the children of God?

Prayer: Lord, help us to open our eyes to see thy will. O God, may we always remember how much thou love us!

My Words Are Eternal
Matthew 24: 34-35

"Verily I say unto you, This generation shall not pass, till all these things be fulfilled. Heaven and earth shall pass away, but my words shall not pass away" (Matthew 24:34-35). There were specific things in this prophecy to transpire at the end of an approximate or limited period of time (this generation shall not pass). However, God's word is not limited in its power or duration. Jesus clearly states here that he knows that our physical heaven and earth will one day cease to be. We should be ready just as those who were warned to be ready in Bible times.

Meditation: What is said in the last book of the Bible about when heaven and earth will pass away?

Prayer: Lord, O God! May we study the scriptures to have knowledge!

Week 45
No One Knows When
Matthew 24: 37-51

"But of that day and hour knoweth no man, no, not the angels of heaven, but my Father only" (Matthew 24:36). Men have attempted to predict when the end of time will occur, but they have failed miserably. When Jesus spoke these words to his disciples, even he did not know the day of the Lord's return. The scripture says "my Father only" knows. It will, therefore, remain a secret, until the day he comes again. We are to be prepared for our Lord's return regardless of when it is!

Meditation: How are we to best prepare for Jesus' return?

Prayer: O God, let us be prepared for thy Son Jesus' return always!

Ten Wise Virgins
Matthew 25:1-13

"Then shall the kingdom of heaven be likened unto ten virgins, which took their lamps, and went forth to meet the bridegroom" (Matthew 25:1). This parable teaches us to be prepared now – today – for the Lord's return. Everyone's lamp should be burning, ready to meet the Lord and pointing to the need to be faithful until the end, until our last breath (Revelation 2:10). No one has a promise of another day. We are

told not to worry or over think tomorrow, but to remember that today is always the day for salvation (Matthew 6:34).

Meditation: Notice the urgency to obey God's instructions, when examining all of the recorded times that people were saved in the scriptures. How soon did they obey after hearing the command to be baptized?

Prayer: O God, please let us take life one day at a time as we prepare for the future.

Don't Hide It
Matthew 25:14-30

"For the kingdom of heaven is as a man travelling into a far country, who called his own servants, and delivered unto them his goods" (Matthew 25:14). Our Christian lights are meant to shine as we travel along the Lord's way. Using the talents entrusted to us, we are to be profitable in his service and by our faith and good works in order to glorify him. It is for the Lord's glory that we best use the talents he has given us.

Meditation: What prompted the unprofitable man to bury his talent?

Prayer: Lord, O God, let us use whatever has been entrusted to us to bring glory to thy name.

Those on His Right
Matthew 25:31-40

"Then shall the King say unto them on his right hand, Come, ye blessed of my Father, inherit the kingdom prepared for you from the foundation of the world" (Matthew 25:34). Here is a future glimpse of King Jesus as he welcomes his loyal servants. This is set to take place after the day of great judgment. Notice that there is also a great separation expressed by those "on his right hand."

Meditation: How does our Lord's promise in John 14:1-3 fit into the idea of a great judgement day?

Prayer: Lord, help us to open our eyes to see thy will O God. Let us be prepared to inherit the place prepared for us!

Those on His Left
Matthew 25:41-46

"Then shall he say also unto them on the left hand, Depart from me, ye cursed, into everlasting fire, prepared for the devil and his angels" (Matthew 25:41). The doctrine of annihilation says that there is no place called hell. This teaching claims that when people die, they cease to exist. This doctrine certainly doesn't fit with the language used here; neither does it fit any New Testament passage. Hell is a real place, an everlasting fire, prepared for those unprepared for eternity.

Meditation: Why do you suppose most will choose a spiritual path leading them to eternal ruin? (See Matthew 7:21.)

Prayer: O God, let us choose wisely while on our earthly journey.

His Own Elect
Luke 18:2-9

"And shall not God avenge his own elect, which cry day and night unto him, though he bears long with them?" (Luke 18:7). Christians are to love their enemies not avenge them. This command is certainly not always easy. God has promised that he would be in charge of retribution. But we often see matters not handled in a faithful manner. Faith is a commodity that seems to be fading from the fabric of human civilization. Hopefully, evidence of faith will be seen until the Lord's return. It will not disappear entirely, as was almost the case in Noah's day when every imagination was only evil continually. We can be very thankful for Noah and his righteous family for saving what was left of humanity from God's wrath and vengeance.

Meditation: What are some ways Christians can love their enemies?

Prayer: O God, let us walk in the light as he is in the light.

Two Men Praying
Luke 18:10-14

"Two men went up into the temple to pray; the one a Pharisee, and the other a publican" (Luke 18:10). Two very different kinds of prayer were prayed that day. The first prayer mentioned was unacceptable. The latter one was accepted and received praise. No matter the position or occupation a person has in life, the heartfelt, penitent prayer of the righteous rises higher than the ceiling. The prophet in Isaiah 59:1-2 mentioned those whose prayers the Lord would not hear. Because of iniquities and sins, people were separated from the Lord. Everyone is in need of God's mercy! When the man of God walks in the light, on the Lord's highway, he is justified before the Lord as was this publican. Verse 9 gives the purpose of the parable—to show that the Pharisees "trusted in themselves that they were righteous."

Meditation: Can a person behave in such a wicked manner that the Lord will refuse to hear his or her prayers?

Prayer: Lord, O God, may we behave ourselves well in thy house!

Week 46
It is Hard for the Rich
Luke 18:18-25

"How hardly shall they that have riches enter into the kingdom of God!" (Luke 18:24). The rich and famous are plagued with many temptations. These seem to be strategically prepared by the enemy and positioned to slay the rich and powerful. Though it is difficult for wealthy individuals to be righteous, it is not impossible. Many rich people of the Bible were also righteous before the Lord including Abraham, Solomon, and Job.

Meditation: What are some of the areas in life particularly difficult for a rich person seeking to be righteous?

Prayer: Lord, help us to open our eyes to see thy will.

Seeking the Lost
Luke 19: 9-10

"This day is salvation come to this house, forasmuch as he also is a son of Abraham. For the Son of man is come to seek and to save that which was lost" (Luke 19: 9-10). Man can be eternally glad that he has a Savior, Christ the Lord, and be exceedingly glad that he was on a rescue mission for the express purpose of saving souls. Jesus still longs for the salvation of souls and has commissioned members of the church today to

be his ministers with him and *"go into all the world to preach the gospel"* (Mark 16:15).

Meditation: Why was the great commission passed along to every faithful Christian?

Prayer: Lord, O God, may we seek and save the lost like Jesus did!

When Jerusalem Is Compassed with Armies

Luke 21:20; 1 Thessalonians 5:2-4; 2 Peter 3:10; Revelations 3:3; Revelation 16:15

"And when ye shall see Jerusalem compassed with armies, then know that the desolation thereof is nigh" (Luke 21:20). This passage brings the context – that the destruction of Jerusalem was imminent – into clearer view. Some seem to point to periodic events today as signs for the imminent coming of the Lord. However, we already know (since that day has been appointed) that the Lord's return is sooner now than when the scriptures were completed sometime around A.D. 68-96. Let's not forget that we cannot know the day or the hour of his return (Matthew 24:36). In this instance, we would do well to remember Noah and what the Bible said about that global event: the world knew nothing until the flood came and took them all away. Today, instead of looking for signs, the dedicated are trimming their lamps to always be a part of the Lord's future plans for the Lord will come "as a thief in the night."

Meditation: What do you suppose the Lord meant when he said he would come "as a thief"?

Prayer: Lord, help us to open our eyes to see thy will.

I am the Vine
John 15:5

"I am the vine, ye are the branches: He that abideth in me, and I in him, the same bringeth forth much fruit: for without me ye can do nothing" (John 15:5). Many people may erroneously believe that by simply doing many good works in the name of the Lord, they can earn a reservation for themselves in heaven. However, going to heaven is not a matter of doing good works alone; it is a matter of having true faith in God. Maintaining good works or fruit is important, and they must mirror a Christ-like attitude and be "through" or "in" Jesus, that is, by his authority (Matthew 7:21-22). We must abide in the vine as a true branch if we are to bear good fruit in him.

Meditation: Explain how faith grows and is demonstrated?

Prayer: Lord, O God, may our faith be what it should be!

I Called You Friends
John 15:15

"Henceforth I call you not servants; for the servant knoweth not what his lord doeth: but I have called you friends; for all things that I have heard of my Father I have made known unto you" (John 15:15). There is no other friend like the loving Jesus. Are you Jesus's friend? And is he yours? Abraham was called the friend of God. If one is a friend of Jesus, then he is also God's friend. If one is in Christ, he is also in Christ's body. Since Christ's body is the church, according to Ephesians 1:22-23, then that person must be a friend of God and of Christ because he is bearing fruit as a member of Christ's church.

Meditation: Why would Jesus call us friends?

Prayer: Lord, O God, may we learn how to be a good friend to our Lord Jesus!

The Spirit of Truth
John 16:13

"Howbeit when he, the Spirit of truth, is come, he will guide you into all truth: for he shall not speak of himself; but whatsoever he shall hear, that shall he speak: and he will show you things to come" (John 16:13). The Holy Spirit shared many truths with Christ's apostles, showing them, in some cases, the future. In fact, he guided them to all truth and inspired all eight New Testament writers, Matthew,

Mark, Luke, John, Peter, Paul, James, and Jude to share with the world the story of Jesus.

Meditation: Why do you suppose we have the story of Jesus' ministry and death from the viewpoint of four different New Testament writers?

Prayer: Lord, help us to learn more about the Holy Spirit.

Jesus Overcomes World
John 16:33

"These things I have spoken unto you, that in me ye might have peace. In the world ye shall have tribulation: but be of good cheer; I have overcome the world." Jesus has overcome the world. Now it's our turn to do the same. He wants all of his disciples to have peace and happiness in him. He has promised each of us the abundant life. Though every Christian will suffer for his commitment to Christ, he will also enjoy the love of God throughout life's challenges.

Meditation: Are there certain steps in overcoming this world? If so, can you think of three?

Prayer: Lord, help us to overcome this world like Jesus did.

Week 47
That They All May Be One
John 17:11, 21

"And now I am no more in the world, but these are in the world, and I come to thee. Holy Father, keep through thine own name those whom thou hast given me, that they may be one, as we are" (John 17:11). Our Lord prayed that all of his apostles would have unity. The term "one" being used is representative of this unity; they should always be "of one mind" in faith. This prayer also extends throughout all subsequent ages to include us, his disciples, that we are united in the same faith and in the same body, the church, (Ephesians 4:1-10)

Meditation: What happens when there is division within someone's household? What is the solution?

Prayer: Lord, help us to be of the "same mind."

Thy Word Is Truth
John 17:17

"Sanctify them through thy truth: thy word is truth" (John 17:17). Before being led to Calvary, Jesus prayed that his disciples would be sanctified (set apart for the Master's use and cleansed from all unrighteousness). The word of God is truth and has power to sanctify us. It cleanses and makes holy all who are unrighteous. Notice Jesus says "through thy

truth." One must actually pass "through the truth." We must allow the truth to authorize what we do for our salvation, for it has the efficacy of sanctification and the power of salvation. Using the truth for instructions in righteousness and obedience, a person can be cleansed and thereby saved.

Meditation: Do you think sanctification is a "once and done" process or a continual process?

Prayer: Lord, teach us to do the things Jesus has commanded us!

Just Two More Days
Matthew 26:2

"You know that after two days is the Passover, and the Son of Man will be delivered up to be crucified" (Matthew 26:2 NKJV). Jesus and his apostles met to share the Feast of the Passover together on Thursday evening, approximately twenty-four hours before Jesus' death. Jesus' betrayal took place soon after the meal had concluded, then his arrest in the garden. Afterwards his trial and hearing began early on Friday morning. He was crucified later that same day and entombed by 6:00 p.m. All of these events happened before the beginning of the Sabbath Day.

Meditation: Why was it important to have Jesus buried before 6:00 p.m.?

Prayer: Dear Lord, thank you for Jesus sacrifice!

She Did a Good Work
Matthew 26:10-13; John 12:8

"For you have the poor with you always, but Me you do not have always" (Matthew 26:11 NKJV). Jesus told his disciples that he would not always be with them. He knew he would soon die on the cross and rise on the third day according to the scriptures. Then he would ascend to the place he was before to be with his Father again. By contrast, Jesus suggests they will have many opportunities to help the poor, since rich and poor people will always exist. There is a way that God's children, in a spiritual sense, can be both poor and rich; they can be poor in spirit and rich in faith.

Meditation: What other lessons could we discover in Jesus' answer?

Prayer: Lord, help us to open our eyes to see thy will.

The Betrayal of Christ
Matthew 26:21-25

"Assuredly, I say to you, one of you will betray me" (Matthew 26:21 NKJV). Jesus knew one of his disciples would betray him, and he knew it would be Judas who would betray him with a kiss. We can clearly recognize the power of God being exercised by Jesus; he knew the future as well as the hearts of men.

Meditation: If Jesus knew what Judas was about to do, then doesn't he know when we are about to sin?

Prayer: Lord, help us to cleanse our hands and hearts.

The Lord's Supper
Matthew 26:26-28; Acts 20:7; 1 Corinthians 16:1-2

"And as they were eating, Jesus took bread, and blessed and broke it, and gave it to the disciples and said, "Take, eat; this is my body. And he took the cup, and gave thanks, and gave it to them, saying, Drink ye all of it; For this is my blood of the new testament, which is shed for many for the remission of sins" (Matthew 26:26-28). At the Feast of the Passover, the Lord's Supper is instituted. After Christ's death and resurrection, it is to be observed by all Christians in the "Christian" or "New Testament" era, also known as the "Last Days." An example of its observance by the early church is found in Acts 20:7, where on this occasion, the first century disciples came together as the church and worshipped. From this passage, as well as, others like 1 Corinthians 16:1-2, we learn that the early disciples came together every first day of the week, to worship and remember the Lord.

Meditation: The early churches were meeting on every first day of the week to contribute and to commune. But why is Sunday the day of worship instead of the Sabbath?

Strike the Shepherd

Matthew 26:31-32; Zechariah 13:7

"All of you will be made to stumble, because of Me this night, for it is written: I will strike the Shepherd and the sheep of the flock will be scattered. But after I have been raised, I will go before you to Galilee" (Matthew 26:31-32 NKJV). The Master again shows his knowledge of future events. Jesus reveals that all of his apostles would soon "stumble" because of him. They would all soon forsake him. He foretells his death by referencing scripture. In this reference, he is the great and loving Shepherd of the sheep. Though he will die, he will also rise again and meet them in Galilee before his departure to heaven.

Meditation: Imagine if you were one of the apostles trying to understand all that Jesus was telling them.

Prayer: Lord, please give us an understanding heart.

Week 48
Jesus Foretells the Exact Moment
Matthew 26:34

"Verily I say unto thee, That this night, before the cock crow, thou shalt deny me thrice" (Matthew 26:34). The future is crystal clear within the viewfinder of the Father; it is not cloudy, vague, or dark. This proves that the Lord had power to clearly see the details of this very specific time of day as to when Peter would deny him, how many times he would do so, and how many times the cock would crow. Peter was very sorry after he denied his Lord and Savior. He wept bitterly and repented. If the Lord can see our mistakes so clearly there is no doubt he also knows of our potential. Later, Peter would become a great preacher on the inaugural day of the church of Christ on the Sunday morning of Pentecost. (Read Mark 14:30.) Peter extended his great leadership when he became an Elder in the Lord's church.

Meditation: Why was Jesus so specific about the exact time of the day that Peter would deny him? Does it help your faith to know that God has that kind of insight and power?

Prayer: Lord, let us come before thee in the sweet hour of prayer.

Watch With Me
Matthew 26:36-38

"Then cometh Jesus with them unto a place called Gethsemane, and saith unto the disciples, Sit ye here, while I go and pray yonder. And he took with him Peter and the two sons of Zebedee, and began to be sorrowful and very heavy. Then saith he unto them, My soul is exceeding sorrowful, even unto death: tarry ye here, and watch with me" (Matthew 26:36-38). Our Lord shows us here that sometimes it is best to be alone when approaching our heavenly Father in prayer and supplication, particularly while asking for guidance. He also shows how valuable close friendships are to our comfort and spiritual progress (Matthew 17:1-9).

Meditation: List at least three ways close friendships might influence our faith. Also consider how having a faithful Christian "spouse" helps one draw closer to the Lord.

Prayer: Lord, teach us how to choose good friends.

Let This Cup Pass
Matthew 26: 39; 2 Corinthians 11: 23-30;
2 Corinthians 12:7-10

"O my Father, if it be possible, let this cup pass from me: nevertheless not as I will, but as thou wilt." (Matthew 26:39). Jesus must have thought it possible that his Father could provide another way for the salvation of mankind. So then, why are we often

reluctant to believe the Lord can make a way for us, when all seems hopeless and impossible? Perhaps we doubt because the answer to Jesus' prayer on this occasion did not provide another way for him. Prayers are answered in various ways; sometimes there seems to be little change in the outcome, but a Christian's prayer is always heard and answered, though it may not be answered as we had first hoped. We must always trust in the Lord's way and in the path he chooses for us. God always has a clear view of the bigger picture and knows just what we need!

Meditation: If someone thinks he has a way to work out a problem should he ask for God's direction and wisdom anyway?

Prayer: Dear God, help us to know that all things are possible with your help.

The Flesh is Weak
Matthew 26:40-41

"What, could ye not watch with me one hour? Watch and pray, that ye enter not into temptation: the spirit indeed is willing, but the flesh is weak" (Matthew 26:40-41). This response from Jesus suggests that his feelings were hurt that his closet friends were sleeping in his most needful hour. Most would argue that they have good intentions, which is a good thing. However, the infirmities, propensities, and weaknesses of the flesh drive us to go to sleep, when we would be better served to "watch and pray" that we might be strong in the Lord (Mark 13:33;14:38).

255

Meditation: Think of an example in your own life when the spirit was willing, but the flesh was weak.

Prayer: Lord, help us to wake up and see thy will.

72,000 Angels
Matthew 26: 52-54

"Put up again thy word into his place: for all they that take the sword shall perish with the sword. Thinkest thou that I cannot now pray to my Father, and he shall presently give me more than twelve legions of angels?" (Matthew 26:52-54). When Jesus was arrested, 72,000 angels were poised, ready if summoned, to come to the aid of our Savior; he had only to ask his Father to send them. God did not force his Son to go to the cross. Jesus had free will just as we do today, and he could have said no. He could have called those legions of angels, changing not only the history of civilization but also the future for all eternity. (See Isaiah 53:7.)

Meditation: Where would we be today if Jesus had chosen to refuse the cross? Do you find it interesting that God, the Father, did not make his Son go to the cross, but rather, Jesus had free will and could have released himself from his impending death?

Prayer: Lord, help us to appreciate more the love of Christ for his Father and for us.

Coming in the Clouds
Matthew 26: 63-66; Psalm 110: 1; Isaiah 53: 7

"Thou hast said: nevertheless I say unto you, Hereafter shall ye see the Son of man sitting on the right hand of power, and coming in the clouds of heaven" (Matthew 26:64). Jesus describes to the High Priest and Jewish leaders, things concerning the destruction of Jerusalem, as well as, the end of time events (Matthew 24:30). In Acts 1:9-11, the Disciples of Christ watched as Jesus ascended in a cloud and were told that he would come again in the same manner in which he ascended. So, on that last hour of that last day, at the sound of the trumpet, he is coming again in the clouds as the righteous meet him in the air.

Meditation: Read farther in the passage cited above and answer the question, why did the high priest tear his clothes after he heard what Jesus said?

Prayer: Lord, help us to live for thee each day!

Earth Shall Pass Away
Mark 13:31; Isaiah 40:8

"Heaven and Earth shall pass away: but my words shall not pass away" (Mark 13:31). The misinformed mistakenly surmise that both the physical heaven and earth will always continue. If they are eternal, as some believe, then people will remain on the earth forever; the seasons will never cease, and the sun and moon will always give their light. Yet Jesus said that heaven and earth will pass away. Since he was with

God from the beginning, he knows the nature of creation (John 1:1-3). There is no scriptural support for the idea of an eternal physical heaven and earth.

Meditation: Since the Bible mentions a new heaven and a new earth Revelation 21:1, could that be the reason some are confused?

Prayer: Lord, help us to remember that thou are not the author of confusion.

Week 49
The New Testament
Mark 14:24-25

"This is my blood of the new testament, which is shed for many" (Mark 14:24). The New Testament was dedicated for everyone, especially for all future believers and validated by Jesus' blood through his death. It takes the blood of Christ to wash or cleanse a person free of his sins, according to Acts 22:16; Romans 6:1-10; 1 Peter 3:21. The New Testament that Jesus refers to here is the new covenant or promise from God. Jews in the first century would contrast it with the old covenant of the Mosaic Law. Of course, the New Testament in our Bibles today did not exist yet in written form when Jesus spoke these words.

Meditation: Why couldn't the blood of bulls and goats take away sin?

Prayer: Lord, help us to open our eyes to see thy will.

Belief and Baptism
Mark 16:15-16

"Go ye into all the world, and preach the gospel to every creature. He that believeth and is baptized shall be saved; but he that believeth not shall be damned" (Mark 16:15-16). Some choose to emphasize the importance of belief and de-emphasize the importance of baptism, while others say the reverse of that is more accurate. But actually, the conjunction *"and"* equalizes and balances both ideas, making them equally important as requirements for one's salvation. Notice that salvation is positioned as the result of a sequence: salvation comes "after" one is baptized, not "before" one is baptized. Every New Testament passage regarding salvation for those becoming Christians follows this sequence, speaking of the achievement of salvation only after a person is biblically baptized into Jesus Christ. Here are three more examples. (Acts 22:16; 1 Peter 3:21; Acts 2:38).

Meditation: If the Bible teaches that one can only be saved after he or she is properly baptized, then why do so many religions teach otherwise?

Prayer: Lord, O God, teach us to respect the proper and commanded order of spiritual things!

Jesus Served Others
Luke 22:26-27

"But ye shall not be so: but he that is greatest among you, let him be as the younger; and he that is chief, as he that doth serve. For whether is greater, he that sitteth at meat, or he that serveth? Is not he that sitteth at meat? But I am among you as he that serveth" (Luke 22:26-27). Jesus says that the greatest person is the one who serves others. Servants will respect others, esteeming them more important than themselves. Jesus said, "Let him be as the younger." It's probable that because Jesus was only 30-33 years old during his ministry that he was younger than some of his apostles. But regardless of any age difference between Jesus and many of his disciples or if any believed he was too young to be a Rabbi (teacher) who had a following of disciples, he served them in many ways by showing that he was the greatest among them. (See Matthew 18:1-6)

Meditation: How does pride affect a child of God's service? Please explain the difference in "service" and "servitude".

Prayer: Lord, O God, may we always humble our hearts before thee!

Eat at My Table

Luke 22:29

"And I appoint unto you a kingdom, as my Father hath appointed unto me; That ye may eat and drink at my table in my kingdom, and sit on thrones judging the twelve tribes of Israel" (Luke 22:29-30). Jesus had instructed his disciples to pray, *"Thy Kingdom come."* He spoke of the kingdom that is here now—his church, the church of Christ. Jesus promised to build or establish the church during his ministry, which occurred on Sunday, the Day of Pentecost some 50 days after his crucifixion. The mention of the "thrones of judging" represents the new era of God's word as the final authority in the judgment of men's souls. The Apostles would help Jesus accomplish his ministry. Today, true Christians everywhere are sharing Christ's purpose and achieving their Father's will. It is the will of God that every servant remember what his Son did on the cross by the observance of the Lord's Supper. The Lord's "table" indicates the Lord's Supper that Christians are to observe on each Lord's Day (Acts 20:7).

Meditation: Why do you suppose some religious people observe the Lord's Supper quarterly and yet schedule their collections weekly? Which Bible passages show the required frequency of these important worship activities?

Prayer: Lord, O God, teach us to rightly divide thy truth!

Satan Desires You
Luke 22:31-32

"Simon, Simon, behold, Satan hath desired to have you, that he may sift you as wheat: but I have prayed for thee, that thy faith fail not: and when thou art converted, strengthen thy brethren" (Luke 22:31-32). It should comfort the Christian today to know that Jesus our Lord and Savior petitions the Father on our behalf. He serves as the mediator between God and man. Jesus once prayed that Simon Peter's faith would not fail and that Peter would receive enough strength to later strengthen his brethren.

Meditation: Is it a good idea to include the same things that Jesus included in his prayer for Peter in our prayers for each other today?

Prayer: Lord, help us to open our eyes to see thy will. O God, may our prayers include those things that will encourage us as well as others!

You Will Not Believe It
Luke 22: 66-70

"If I tell you, ye will not believe: And if I also ask you, ye will not answer me, nor let me go. Hereafter shall the Son of man sit on the right hand of the power of God" (Luke 22:67-70). The elders of the people, chief priests and scribes, had asked him if he were the Christ, the Son of God. They did not believe, even with Jesus standing before them face-to- face, both saying

it and showing that he was indeed the Christ, the son of God (vs. 70). People behave similarly today as they did in the first century. Some are slow to believe, while others respond favorably. (See Hebrews 1:3.)

Meditation: Why do you think this segment of the population, the elders and scribes, were slow to believe?

Prayer: Lord, let us not be slow to trust and obey thee.

Daughters of Jerusalem
Luke 23:28-31

"Daughters of Jerusalem, weep not for me, but weep for yourselves, and for your children" (Luke 23:28). There would be troublesome times ahead for Jewish women and their children. Jesus said for them to be more concerned for themselves than for him. During the time of Christ's birth, Herod had killed many children, hoping to end Jesus' life. Certainly, we are justifiably concerned today with the world's climate of immorality and social injustices. We remain hopeful and eager for a safe and loving environment for our children and for the generations to come.

Meditation: What did Hosea, the prophet say in Hosea 4:6 concerning why a whole nation of people were destroyed? Why would that have caused many to weep?

Prayer: Lord, let us open eyes to see what is around us.

Week 50
Jesus Prays for Future Believers
John 17:20-26

"Neither pray I for these alone, but for them also which shall believe on me through their word" (John 17:20). Several years after his prayer, his disciples would be called Christians for the first time at Antioch (Acts 11:26). Our Lord prayed here for disciples in the first century and for all future disciples who would be called Christians.

Meditation: Do you think Jesus was including us, 21st century Christians, in his prayer?

Prayer: Lord, O God, let us pray for all the future Christians!

Son of Man Must Be Crucified
Luke 24:1-9; Isaiah 53

"The Son of man must be delivered into the hands of sinful men, and be crucified, and the third day rise again" (John 24:7). It had always been his Father's plan for Jesus to suffer and die by crucifixion. After Jesus' agonizing prayer in Gethsemane, he told John that he would drink the cup that his Father had prepared for him. Jesus' death and resurrection had

been prophesied in so many of the Messianic prophesies of old.

Meditation: Why does Jesus pray for unity among all true believers? What hinders us from achieving unity?

Prayer: Lord, O God, let us endeavor to keep our unity!

Behold My Glory
John 17:24

"Father, I will that they also, whom thou hast given me, be with me where I am; that they may behold my glory, which thou hast given me: for thou lovedst me before the foundation of the world" (John 17:24). Christians often sing today that the Lord will be with us. One such popular hymn written by Sanderson in 1935 is almost like a prayer:

> Be with me, Lord I cannot live without Thee,
> I dare not try to take one step alone;
> I cannot bear the loads of life unaided,
> I need Thy strength to lean myself upon.

John records that Jesus expresses desire for the Christian to be with him where he is. The idea is that if love existed to be given before the foundation of the world, it will also exist after the world's end. Jesus longs for his disciples to see the glory that the Father has given him! (See John 14:1-3.)

Meditation: Do you think Peter, James, and John witnessed that glory to some degree during Jesus' transfiguration on the mountain? What about during Jesus' ascension?

Prayer: Lord, help us to open our eyes to see thy glory! May we let our own lights shine so that others may see thee through us!

Christ in Me
John 17:25-26

"O righteous Father, the world hath not known thee: but I have known thee, and these have known that thou hast sent me. And I have declared unto them thy name, and will declare it: that the love wherewith thou hast loved me may be in them and I in them" (John 17:25-26). The world seems, in general, to be uninterested or unmotivated to know about spiritual things in general, beginning with our physical origin through Adam and now our spiritual birth in Christ. Not only is Christ in us when we become Christians, but also the Father's love is in us. In Romans 5:5 we read *"And hope maketh not ashamed; because the love of God is shed abroad in our hearts by the Holy Ghost which is given unto us."*

Meditation: Since knowledge is a key to understanding God, shouldn't it be a priority for us to read and meditate on those things that God has written?

Prayer: Lord, O God, give us a heart that is motivated to understand more of thee!

Put Away Your Sword
John 18:11; Matthew 26:36-42

"Put up the sword into the sheath: the cup which my Father hath given me, shall I not drink it?" (John 18:11). This is the same cup that Jesus prayed, while he was in Gethsemane, that might be taken away from him; however, he resolved to drink that cup of anguish and save believers from their sins. One should never take his own sword to fight against the sword of the Spirit – the word of God. The will of the Father was for his Son to suffer on the cross, not to be rescued from it. Jesus could have called thousands of angels to rescue him, but how then could he have become our much needed Savior?

Meditation: Could the cup mentioned in this passage foreshadow the fact that followers of Christ today will have difficult things that they must face in their own lives? What might be in the cup of the faithful?

Prayer: Lord, may you give us courage to drink from the cup of thy choosing. Help us to learn more about Jesus' life and death!

Said Nothing in Secret
John 18:19-23

"If I have spoken evil, bear witness of the evil: but if well, why smitest thou me?" (John 18:23). Jesus taught openly to the world. He consistently taught in the synagogues and in the temple of the Jews. Though he did at times speak privately to his closest disciples,

he did not speak secretively about those things that could save men. This passage proves that those today who claim Jesus had a secret message – another revelation or document that wasn't shown to everyone – couldn't possibly be correct, because their claim is not backed by credible evidence or scripture.

Meditation: What can we read in Galatians chapter one that warns us about teaching another kind of Gospel?

Prayer: Lord, help us to open our eyes to see thy will, O God!

The King of the Jews
John 18:36; John 6:15

"My kingdom is not of this world: if my kingdom were of this world, then would my servants fight, that I should not be delivered to the Jews: but now is my kingdom not from hence" (John 18:36). The church, or kingdom, is not from this earth. Jesus gives us an important insight into his kingdom, in that it exists on earth, but is not ultimately an earthly kingdom. If it had been an earthly kingdom his disciples would have fought all the necessary battles. Some want to make it a physical realm with its throne in literal Jerusalem; but the Lord's kingdom is a spiritual one that doesn't have the earth as its foundation or eternal location.

Meditation: What are some other differences in a spiritual kingdom and a physical one?

Prayer: Lord, may we seek thee with our whole hearts.

Week 51
What Is Truth?
John 18:37

"Thou sayest that I am a king. To this end was I born, and for this cause came I into the world, that I should bear witness unto the truth. Every one that is of the truth heareth my voice" (John 18:37). After this thought provoking statement from Jesus, Pilate asks the question, "What is truth?" This is possibly one of the most important questions ever asked by a man. The religious world had been searching for truth for ages. Pilate discovered that Jesus was always the perfect piece of the prophesied puzzle. Jesus said in John 14:6 that he was "the truth." (Read John 17:17-20.)

Meditation: If people are still searching for the truth today then why haven't they found it?

Prayer: Lord, help us to rightly divide that divine truth.

After Three Days
Matthew 27:63; 28:10

"After three days I will rise again" (Matthew 27:63). *"Be not afraid: go tell my brethren that they go into Galilee, and there shall they see me"* (28:10). Here, our Lord does not predict (a prediction has a rate or percentage of failure); instead, he prophesies (words that are 100% accurate with absolutely no fail rate) that he would rise from the dead on the third day. That day, very early in the morning, would be a Sunday—the first day of the week. Later, we find his disciples worshipping on that day and observing his supper in remembrance of that special event. (See Matthew 27:19-23; Acts 20:7.)

Meditation: Why might those who first saw Jesus after his resurrection not recognize him?

Prayer: Lord, help us to remember what Jesus did for us.

Father Forgive Them
Luke 23:34; 2 Timothy 3:7

"Father, forgive them; for they know not what they do" (Luke 23:34). Ignorance plays a significant role in our religious environment today. Jesus showed mercy to those who cried out, "Crucify him, crucify him!" He showed mercy to the Romans for having him put to death instead of releasing him. Some say the Father answered his Son's prayer 50 days later on Pentecost when many asked what they should do for their forgiveness (Acts 2:37).

Meditation: Since it takes time to acquire knowledge, what should a person do in the meantime while he or she is still largely ignorant?

Prayer: Lord, O God, may we grow in the knowledge of thee!

My God, My God!
Mark 15:34; Psalm 22:1, 6-8

ELOI, ELOI, LAMA SABACHTHANI?. . . My God, my God, why hast thou forsaken me?" (Mark 15:34). Because Jesus, in this moment, bore the sins of the whole world, his loving Father had to look away, even if only for a moment; and Jesus bore his agonizing pain and suffering upon the cross all alone.

Meditation: Today how does sin separate man from God? (See Isaiah 59:1-2.)

Prayer: Lord, let not our sins cause thee to look away.

The Thief on the Cross
Luke 23:43

"Verily I say unto thee, Today shalt thou be with me in paradise" (Luke 23:43). It is certainly the case that we are saved by faith, but many New Testament passages also teach us that baptism is an important part of our faith. Baptism, which means immersion, is a commandment required to be obeyed before a person is legitimately saved and added to the church

(Acts 2:47). In 1 Peter 3:21, we learn as a matter of doctrine that "baptism now saves us."

Immersion in water in the name of the Father, Son, and Holy Spirit wasn't necessary before Christ's death upon the cross. In fact, it wasn't even available! The baptism that now saves us does so by the cleansing power of the blood of Jesus Christ. It took the death of Christ and the shedding of his blood to make this special kind of baptism possible. It first came into use 50 days after the death of Jesus on the Day of Pentecost (Acts 2:1). On that Sunday morning, the gospel message rang out and about 3,000 people were baptized for the remission of sins (Acts 2:38).

Though this baptism was not available to the thief prior to our Lord's death, burial, and resurrection, mercy was available. The thief confessed his sin. Recognizing that Jesus was being punished unjustly, the thief asked Jesus to remember him in his kingdom. Jesus had the power and authority to forgive sins while on earth, and so Jesus told the former thief that he would be with him in Paradise that day.

Some Bible scholars believe it was highly probable that the thief had earlier been baptized with John's baptism. Mark 1:5 says, "*And there went out unto him [John] all the land of Judea, and they of Jerusalem, and were all baptized of him in the River of Jordan, confessing their sins.*" By his words on the cross, it seems that the thief had knowledge of John's teachings. It also seems that he knew something about Jesus, for he said, "*This man hath done nothing amiss*" (Luke 23:41). By this logic, he finally confesses his sins on the cross and calls Jesus "Lord," thereby finishing the process that was initiated after he believed and was baptized by John. (See Luke 23:33-43.)

Meditation: Why do some people point to the thief on the cross to defend their doctrinal position that baptism is not required for salvation? Why do they refuse all the other scriptures that teach that baptism is required?

Prayer: Lord, let us consider all of thy words carefully.

Into Thy Hands
Luke 23:44-47

"Father, into thy hands I commend my spirit" (Luke 23:46). "Into thy hands" means into the Father's authority and safe keeping. God the Father is the Father of all spirits. When one dies, his spirit leaves his body and returns to the Father who gave it to that person in the first place. The meaning here is that we cannot direct our own spirit into one place or another after death, but it is up to the God of heaven as to where the spirit will go after leaving the body. Our actions (faithfulness) before death will influence the direction of our spirits after death.

Meditation: If the spiritual part of the mind dwells in the mind, why is it described as being the "heart of man?"

Prayer: Lord, help us to open our minds to understand thy will. O God, may we with all our hearts serve thee.

What Is the Discussion?
Luke 24:17

"What manner of communications are these that ye have one to another, as ye walk, and are sad?" (Luke24:17). Jesus already knew the answer to the question he asks here. He asks of his disciples, "What are you discussing as you're walking together so sadly?" This reminds us that the Lord is also aware of every subject under discussion today. No thought, word, or deed goes unnoticed. It is also noteworthy to point out that Christ addresses their frame of mind. Many instances of joy and sadness exist today, and the Lord is aware of them all!

Meditation: Isn't it important for people to know what makes them unhappy and what gives them joy? How should a Christian feel when the Lord's name is taken in vain?

Prayer: Lord, help us to guard our tongues from evil. May our lips speak without guile!

Week 52

Touch Me and See
Luke 24:39

"Behold my hands and my feet, that it is I myself: handle me and see; for a spirit hath not flesh and bones, as ye see me have" (Luke 24:39). The apostle John writes later in 1 John 1:1 that his hand was among many that had personally cared for the Savior.

He begins in this way to present the eyewitness testimony of the death and resurrection of the Son of God; yet even so, some are slow of heart to believe. (See 1 Corinthians 15:1-10.)

Meditation: Why was it so important for the apostles and others to have the experience of witnessing Jesus in the flesh?

Prayer: Lord, help us to close our eyes that we might truly see! Keep us in thy love, oh God!

David Wrote About Me
Luke 24:44; Hebrews 10:19-20

"These are the words which I spake unto you, while I was yet with you, that all things must be fulfilled, which were written in the Law of Moses, and in the prophets, and in the psalms, concerning me" (Luke 24:44). Jesus Christ's coming fulfilled the first covenant – the Law of Moses – and established and probated the new covenant, or New Testament. A new and better testament was established because Jesus was a new and better sacrifice than any of the animals used in prior sacrificial or consecration ceremonies (ceremonies involving sprinkling of blood).

Meditation: Why was the old covenant called the Law of Moses? Did any of the Ten Commandments carry over to become part of the New Covenant? How were people saved under the old system? How are they saved today?

Prayer: Lord, let us desire to read thy word carefully. Create in us an open heart and mind.

Repentance and Remission
Luke 24: 46-49

"Thus it is written, and thus it behooved Christ to suffer, and to rise from the dead the third day: And that repentance and remission of sins should be preached in his name among all nations, beginning at Jerusalem. And ye are witnesses of these things. And, behold, I send the promise of my Father upon you: but tarry ye in the city of Jerusalem, until ye be endued with power from on high" (Luke 24:46-49). Both repentance and remission of sins should be preached today, especially since 50 days after his death and resurrection, those things were preached at Pentecost. On that day, Peter said, "Repent and be baptized every one of you in the name of Jesus Christ for the remission of sins..." (Acts 2:38). According to every biblical example of people being saved, remission of sins always follows a scriptural baptism (Acts 2:1-11; Acts 8: 26-40).

Meditation: Since "repentance and remission of sins" was the message of the first-century conversions, shouldn't it still be the message preached today?

Prayer: Lord, O God, teach us to know how our sins are forgiven!

The Great Commission
Matthew 28:18-20

"All power is given unto me in heaven and in earth. Go ye therefore, and teach all nations, baptizing them in the name of the father, and of the Son, and of the Holy Ghost: Teaching then to observe all things whatsoever I have commanded you: and, lo, I am with you always, even unto the end of the world. Amen" (Matthew 28:18-20). The Great Commission is great for a number of reasons. First, its scope is great because it encompasses every nation. Second, it is great because it shares the Lord's plan of salvation with all of creation by laying out the path each must walk to claim citizenship in the church. Jesus clearly states the things that a person must do to be saved as he begins a long-term relationship with the Savior. The commission is also great because it provides a pattern for faithfulness throughout every generation. (Read 1 Peter 3:21; Acts 22:16; Mark 16:16; Acts 2:37-38; Acts 8:36-42.)

Meditation: Since people responded favorably to the gospel of Jesus and met the requirements to be saved in each example recorded in the Bible, shouldn't individuals who do the same today also be saved?

Prayer: Lord, help us to open our eyes to see thy will. O God, teach us thy plan for our salvation!

Doubting Thomas
John 20:27-29

"...Reach hither thy finger, and behold my hands; and reach hither thy hand, and thrust it into my side: and be not faithless, but believing ... Thomas, because thou hast seen me thou hast believed: blessed are they that have not seen and yet have believed" (John 20:27-29). Unlike Thomas, the Lord's faithful followers today do not have to see him to know him. Faith is invisible, but it is never blind. (Read Hebrews 11:1, 6.)

Meditation: What are some examples today of being faithless? Since faith is required to be saved, what might we infer about an unsaved person?

Prayer: Lord, O God, teach us to increase our faith.

Feed My Sheep
John 21:15

"Simon, son of Jonas, lovest thou me more than these? . . . . Feed my lambs" (John 21:15). Just seven weeks following his death, the apostle Simon Peter would be the Lord's spokesman on Sunday morning, the Day of Pentecost. He would preach the love story of the cross to an approximate crowd of 1,000,000 Jews that had converged on Jerusalem for the festival. Some years later, Simon would become a beloved shepherd to a congregation of Christ's church – a church of Christ (Romans 16:16). Along with other elders of the local church, he would have the responsibility of feeding the Lord's sheep by ensuring that the congregation had a steady diet of God's word

to help the flock grow and remain faithful (John 8:32).

Meditation: How much love does it require to want to teach someone the gospel of Jesus Christ? Please study the meaning of the terms shepherd, elder and pastor. What leadership qualities do each signify.

Prayer: Lord, O God, teach us to love one another.

Follow Me, until I Come Again
John 21:22

"Jesus saith unto him, If I will that he tarry till I come, what is that to thee? Follow thou me" (John 21:22). Interestingly, the four gospels close in the same way they open - with Jesus inviting us to follow him. Jesus commands Peter to follow him regardless of what he had planned for John. It is a good lesson for those of us who look around and gauge the importance of our own service by basing it on what others may or may not be accomplishing for Jesus themselves. We are told in the Bible that it is unwise to compare ourselves with others. We should look to Jesus and accomplish whatever he has planned for us to do, regardless of what others may or may not be doing for him. At the same time, we should not have the mindset that we will venture off forever being alone in our convictions. Being a team player, as opposed to a lone ranger, is more in keeping with the theme of New Testament Christianity. (See 2 Corinthians 10:12.)

Meditation: Is it possible to allow the successes and failures of others to hinder our work for the Master?

Prayer: Lord, help us to pay attention to your will for us! Teach us to always be busy in thy kingdom, oh God!

DAY 365

What Did Jesus Say About How a Person is Saved Today!

Please read everything Jesus said below and do them to be saved (Luke 6:46)!
- Hear the Gospel and Believe (John 3:16).
- Repent (Luke 13:3, 5).
- Confess Him (Matthew 10:32).
- Be Baptized (Mark 16:16, Acts 2:38, Acts 22:16, 1 Peter 3:21).

Saved persons are added to his church (Acts 2:47; Ephesians 4:4, 5; Ephesians 1, 22, 23).

Saved persons must be faithful and do the Father's will (Matthew 7:21; Revelation 2:10).

*Dear Friend, thank you so much for reading this book! It is my hope that it will help you in some meaningful way as you follow the Savior's plan for a Christian life. Please let me know what you think. God Bless!

Works Cited

Davey, Mark. "Alcohol." *The Drug Data Series.* An Information Sheet from the National Drug & Alcohol Statistics Unit, Australia. 14 Sep 1998.<http://www.powerup.com.au/~md avey/alco hol.htm>.

ERV, Easy –To- Read Version. Translated from the Original Languages. New Testament Bible. Fort Worth: World Bible Translation Center, 2005. Print.

KJV, King James Version Bible. Vereeniging: Christian Arts Publisher,2016. Print.

Sanderson, Lloyd. O. "Be With Me, Lord". *Sacred Selections For The Church,* 1935.

Smith's Bible Dictionary, Nashville, TN: Holman, 1991.

The American Heritage Dictionary of the English Language/High-School Edition. Boston: Houghton Mifflin Company, 1982.

Made in the USA
Columbia, SC
22 October 2024

44448877R00169